Total Freedom

Total Freedom

Experiencing Supernatural Victory
Through Jesus Christ

Armour and Siola McFarland

Total Freedom

ISBN: 978-1-257-95890-0

Published by Total Freedom Fellowship

Disclaimer: all names have been changed in this book to protect individual identities. There is no intent to slander any person.

Dedication

We give thanks to our Heavenly Father
for Armour J. McFarland, husband,
father, and Pastor.

He had the spirit of obedience to pioneer
into an area the LORD Jesus had planned for him
before he was born, opening the door to
a ministry giving our LORD the opportunity
to snatch many from the fire.

Jude 1:23

Special Note from Siola

The following pages will give you courage and spiritual energy from our Heavenly Father as you read true stories of direct battle with the enemy. It is my desire to share with you practical ways the LORD Jesus has taught Armour and me to combat the enemy and win. These practical ways will help you become strong and victorious like Joshua. You will experience success over the enemy as he attempts to keep you from arriving at the anointed place God chose for you before the beginning of time.

As you read the scriptures and use the prayers provided to push the enemy out of the way, you will be delighted in fully experiencing the TOTAL FREEDOM the LORD Jesus makes available. This is not something new, it has always been in the Word of God, but Satan has strategically placed veils to blind spiritual eyes. He causes the body of Christ to set aside and ignore the vital mandate Jesus gave His disciples and us as modern day disciples to continue this ministry.

Nothing has changed since the day Jesus passed the baton to his men to proceed with his teachings. The instructions to us are the same. God has not changed. Jesus has not changed. His Word has not changed.

It is our purpose to pass on the steps the Holy Spirit deposited with us. Maybe you have been in Christian circles and sensed something was not complete. Something was missing. The power was gone. You have been looking for a missing puzzle piece that will ignite your life.

God desires for you to experience the taste of conquering the enemy. The invisible spiritual forces in your life will disappear as freedom is found. The chains that have kept you bound will be broken and the bondage you have known will disappear, all in the name and the blood of Jesus.

Now the LORD is the Spirit, and where the Spirit of the LORD is, there is freedom.
2 Corinthians 3:17

Siola McFarland

CONTENTS

Introduction   11

1. Our First Night   19

2. Our Second Encounter   23

3. Depend on God for Angelic Protection   33

4. Encounters in the Visiting Room   41

5. Deliverance by Phone   49

6. The Blood of Jesus   57

   Blood of Jesus at an Abortion Clinic   58

   Blood of Jesus Protects on Vacation   59

   Voices in the Night   60

   Spiritual Warfare Prayer   65

   Spiritually Cleansing Your Home   66

   Covering Medications   68

   Covering Internal Systems   69

   Cleansing the House and the Land   70

7. Declaring War Against the Enemy 75

    Punishments 77

    Commands 78

    Prayer to Break Witchcraft Curses 79

8. An Amazing God 81

9. Do Not Be Ignorant of Satan's Devices 97

10. The Word of God 111

    Scripture to Use Against the Enemy 139

    Scripture to Combat Fear 144

    Scripture for Deliverance 146

Appendix A: Rearrange Your World 151

Appendix B: Phrases to Assist in Warfare
                Praying 155

Acknowledgments 157

Introduction

As authors we have been exposed to spiritual warfare for over thirty years. It is our desire to provide a practical, easy to understand manual on spiritual warfare so you, as a soldier of Jesus Christ, are trained to use spiritual weapons. We are confident young and old alike can successfully achieve victory against attacks from the enemy. May you be encouraged to ask the LORD to help you see with His eyes.

The heart of true spiritual warfare is to love and forgive those who badger you, those who enjoy putting you down, those who appear to be jealous of you and talk about you, and those who knowingly or unknowingly send you verbal curses. These are everyday attacks. With God's help we are to love the attacker. A Godly perspective is important.

There is a gut level of hatred we must have, but it is only focused on the unseen forces of the enemy. Satan's strategy is to use people who are around us to keep us from fulfilling God's purpose in our lives.

"Do I not hate them, O LORD, who hate you? And do I not loathe those who rise up against you? I hate them with perfect hatred; I count them my enemies." *Psalm 139: 21,22*

We believe spiritual warfare has been presented in Christian circles in a way that has caused many people to fear. People reason since Satan has so much power he cannot be overcome by an everyday believer. This book is designed to show you how to successfully take authority over the enemy and win. You can know how to get the monkey off your back and experience victory again and again as you face the obstacles of the enemy.

Many students of the WORD have chosen other areas of study because they have not had true deliverance modeled by their leaders. They have not seen people set completely free from addictions, from the enemy's harassment, or free from situations that are continually holding them back. We have been led to think only learned scholars can enter this area of ministry and successfully manage this subject. It is a lie from the enemy.

David conquered a giant, not because of the courses he studied online, and he didn't learn confrontational combat from the soldiers in Saul's palace in order to master the weapons of that day. Yet he knew no fear. His training came when he had killed a lion and a bear while in charge of his father's sheep. He was prepared in his heart to fight the opposition and to stand with courage on the promises of God. He knew God in real life situations and had seen Him come to the rescue time and time again.

In this book we will share what the Holy Spirit has revealed to us. We found Him to be a very orderly teacher. Through the WORD, the Holy Spirit brought to our understanding more of Jesus' teaching, including deliverance and healing which had not been covered during our years at Christian college or in seminary training. It was also not evident in the churches where we participated. We will bring forth what the LORD taught us in our home, and verified in with His WORD. You will read of the freedom many have come to experience as a result of obeying and applying His WORD.

We will share with you how an invisible fortress against the enemy can be felt and seen by satanic forces, and also how the LORD graciously led us to develop a ministry that would help individuals become free from the enemy's grip. Many people are now finding Jesus to be their Deliverer as well as Savior. This dimension of ministry is often avoided because of fear.

Some teach warfare as a biblical principle but not as one who has faced a demon head on and known what to do. Others use a fly – swatter approach where they may lay hands on an individual, then proceed to command every evil spirit in the person to leave. In this book we will show how patience, dependence on the Holy Spirit's guidance, and an understanding of the fundamentals from the Word of God will help to produce great results and enable the individual to maintain the ground that has been gained.

We believe many have gone into ministry without receiving deliverance from past strongholds. As a result, they have carried baggage into the pulpit without personally experiencing freedom in those areas. Often churches fail to equip Christians in handling the attacks of Satan. We have met those who do not believe they are in a war at all. In turn they have accepted a false teaching from the doctrines of demons that one can survive in the world by living a form of Christianity.

It is not uncommon for a pastor to relinquish his pastoral role to a professional counselor. However, this counselor is not allowed to remove any demonic entities from the life of a tormented person because of the oaths taken at the time of licensure. Instead, he prescribes medication to remove symptoms and bring temporary relief. Unfortunately, it does not eliminate the root of the problem like Jesus taught His disciples to do. This is bondage not freedom.

One Christian family counseling service called our home asking if our ministry would help a college student they had been working with for some time. The staff admitted being unable to go any further with her using their treatments and wanted to refer the young woman to us for continued work. They believed what she needed now was deliverance from evil spirits and wondered if we would consider meeting and praying with her to set her free. Since they represented a Christian counseling service we asked why they were not supplying that help. They said their license did not allow them to minister in this fashion and they simply had no idea how to proceed.

Jesus did not need a psychological approach to help an individual. We need to get back to the basics, review how Jesus trained his men, and then follow his direction. Jesus wants us to know what to do in this area and also to be active in it. This is not an option. It is a mandate to every believer.

He said to them, "GO INTO ALL THE WORLD AND PREACH the good news to all creation. Whoever believes and is baptized will be saved, but whoever does not believe will be condemned. AND THESE SIGNS WILL ACCOMPANY THOSE WHO BELIEVE: In my name they will drive out

demons; they will speak in new tongues; they will pick up snakes with their hands; and when they drink deadly poison, it will not hurt them at all; they will place their hands on sick people, and they will get well." *Mark 16:15-18*

The body of Christ needs to come together and practice what was a core feature in the New Testament Church. Is the use of oil omitted in your church when praying for the sick? When leaders avoid using oil and the laying on of hands, we are forgetting the effectiveness and fundamental practice of the original church. Many churches have deviated from God's original plan to deliver and to heal; yet, the Holy Spirit has not changed. We tend to rely on the medical doctors to heal instead of the priestly position given by God, which is vital to the life and the body of Christ.

It is easy to use the excuse that miracles and healings were eliminated after the last disciple of Christ died, and that Mark 16:17-20 was not to have been included in the Bible. There are those who believe it was printed in error. In my experience, the LORD has shown that His WORD is true and not a mistake. Even if these verses were not included, there remains more than enough evidence to prove that the LORD expects us to be unusual, to be prepared for battle, and to be courageous and brave. We are to trust in His Word, and experience and expect victory every time we engage against the enemy.

Jesus provided everything we need at the cross. It has been done. It is at our disposal. The name of Jesus is powerful and his blood continues to flow today. Each one of us is preparing the way for Jesus to return by accomplishing feats He said would be greater than His. It is awesome to move ahead in Jesus' name until that day when He returns in full victory.

This manual is not the last word on deliverance, nor does it encompass everything that can be learned in this area. However, we are excited to make available practical ways to take authority over the evil one and his cohorts, and with angelic support demolish kingdoms and his schemes. We are all end-time warriors in a battle for such a time as this.

In this manual:

- You will learn how to discern the attacks of the enemy on an individual. As you submit to the guidance of the Holy Spirit you will learn strategies to eliminate and demolish the plans Satan is using to rob you of God's blessings.

- Godly confidence will replace the fear that lack of knowledge brings. This manual will also help dissolve fears you may have in combating the enemy. No matter how young or how old you are it is imperative that you experience victory over Satan on a daily basis.

- You will learn how to call on our Father in heaven to send specific angelic assistance and protection. The Word of God contains many punishments, which through prayer God will bring down to destroy the kingdom of Satan.

- You will learn what the Word of God says about being a fighter in His army and how we can encourage others to join in the fight. Through the years, I have continued this ministry even after my husband's graduation to Glory. We continue to train people in deliverance and give God all the Glory. He is the One that sets a prisoner free.

1

Our First Night

By Armour

It was a quiet summer evening in the late seventies. My wife and I had just left a church sponsored youth event highlighting the dangers of delving into the world of the occult. My Seminary training never equipped me for what I was to experience that night, but it was the beginning of what would be an amazing journey.

I have always been passionate for young people and seeing them come to the LORD, but that evening we encountered a teenager who had not made the choice to follow Jesus Christ, but instead had opened the door to a realm that was attempting to pull him down forever.

In our conversation with this young man, we soon recognized we were in a situation similar to the story of

Jesus and the man in the tombs. After the initial shock, we both realized what was happening. We were face to face with someone controlled by a demon. A different voice, personality and supernatural strength emerged. Our shock quickly faded as we became angry at Satan and his demons.

My wife and I had met at a conservative Christian college and we were both quite naïve. In all the training I had in theology and education, and in the classes we attended, the subject of equipping Christians to battle against demonic forces was not dealt with. We did not learn how to rescue a person from the grips of Satan. But now, with the Holy Spirit as our teacher, it was as if the Holy Spirit was saying, "Fasten your seatbelts for I am going to show you what is really going on in lives around you."

Yes, we were naïve that night, but our anger far exceeded our lack of understanding. We began a relentless attack through the power of God. In the name of Jesus Christ and by His shed blood, we commanded the demons to come out!

The long battle we faced that evening was a physical and spiritual challenge. Not only did it change our paradigm on the power accessible through the blood of Jesus to all believers, it gave us a much clearer picture of how passionately Satan desires to steal, kill and destroy lives, relationships, marriages, God given dreams, and our future hope in Jesus Christ.

As a result of that encounter, we were more committed than ever to walk the path God was placing before us, and to assist individuals harassed, bound, oppressed, and enslaved by the prince of darkness. We have learned much since that First Night and in this book we will give you a glimpse into a few of the many similar encounters that arose over the years. There are simple strategies that make the battle more efficient so we can all experience continued victories in Jesus' name. Join us as we share more clearly how to enjoy total freedom.

In review:

- The Name of Jesus and the Blood of Jesus is a strong weapon against the enemy.
- Hold your position on the battlefield. The victory is the Lords.
- Don't retreat. Stand firm. The LORD fights your battles.
- Neither my wife nor myself were hurt in this encounter.
- No matter how the enemy tries to intimidate you or to weaken your position, don't pay attention. Stay focused.

There is nothing like freedom.

2

Our Second Encounter

By Armour

When we shared the story of our First Night with the people at church, a Christian nurse was in attendance. A few days later, she got a call from a young lady who was attempting to commit suicide. The nurse answered the cry for help and then gave us a call.

"I'm working with a young lady that seems to have the same problems the young man you told us about experienced. Can you come over and help me right away?"

We didn't know how to answer her. We were not experts in dealing with these spirits and only had one night of experience. We could offer no special suggestions to help out with another encounter.

The nurse shared that this girl was not a Christian and she would like to receive Jesus Christ as her personal Savior. However, she hears voices that won't let her do it and claim they will kill her if she does.

We did know what it meant to receive Jesus Christ as your Savior and told her we would pray and be there as quickly as possible. It was a Saturday afternoon and we were free from other responsibilities.

My wife and I prayed as we drove the five miles to the young lady's upstairs apartment. We knocked on the door and the nurse came down to let us in.

It took no more than two minutes for us to head back up the stairs, but by the time we got to her living quarters, the girl was sitting in the middle of her bed with a long towel knotted around her neck. She was pulling on both ends trying to kill her self by chocking off her air.

She was hardly breathing.

The nurse quickly grabbed the towel and struggled to loosen it. The girl tried to fight off the nurse. After a short tussle, the nurse freed the towel and the girl began to breathe normally again.

As we sat down near the bed we began to talk to the girl, Suzanne, and asked some questions. She was very sullen at first and didn't want to talk. Finally she broke down and began to answer our questions.

Yes, she knew about Jesus Christ, but she had never received Him as her Savior. We talked with her a few minutes about who Jesus was and what He had done for her in dying on the cross. Then we asked her if she would like to receive Him as her personal Savior this afternoon?

She said something that startled us, "Yes, I would like to, BUT THE VOICES I AM HEARING TELL ME THEY WILL KILL ME IF I DO."

Here again our anger at Satan began to boil. What right did Satan have to try and destroy the opportunity for this girl to be saved from her sins?

We asked her a little about her background. She was a witch and had been heavily involved with séances. She was scheduled to travel to a neighboring state to be initiated as a bride of Satan in a special ceremony within the next week. The voices also gave her great guilt about a recent death in her family.

Suzanne said she wanted out, but the VOICES threatened her and would not let her go. She knew what demons were. She had been using them in her witchcraft practices, but she didn't know of a way to escape from them.

We finally said, "In the name of Jesus we want to speak to the voices." We stated just once, "In the name of Jesus, you voices that have been bothering Suzanne, identify yourself and speak through her mouth."

A low range, masculine voice came from her mouth,

"What do you want?"

We commanded, "In the name of Jesus, who are you? Give us your name. What right do you have to be in her body?"

The voice replied very clearly, "My name is "Old Dad," and I have a right to be here because she will not forgive."

I said, "What do you mean, she won't forgive? Who won't she forgive?"

The "Old Dad" voice said, "She won't forgive Bruce, James, and her dad."

The "Old Dad" voice continued, "I don't have to leave her because she will not forgive. The Bible says so in Matthew 18."

We turned to Matthew 18 and read the story of the unforgiving servant and how God said the king turned the unforgiving servant over to the tormentors until the debt was paid.

We said, "Are you saying that God turns people over to the torment of demons?"

The voice replied, "Exactly, and I don't have to do a thing you say because she will not forgive."

Then we commanded, "In the name of Jesus, Old Dad, we don't want to talk to you any more right now. We want to talk to Suzanne."

Here I must comment to help you understand that in some cases, as with the young teenager on our First Night, the individual being plagued by these spirits could not hear any of the conversation going on until the deliverance prayers were ended. There was a similarity in this case as well. This does not have to be the pattern in every case.

"We want to talk to this young lady's own personality. Move aside, Old Dad, we want to talk with Suzanne."

In an instant, Suzanne's personality was back. Suzanne was not aware of the conversation that took place. It was as if she had been in another room and now was with us again. We heard the difference in her voice and knew she was back. We could tell she knew nothing about what the demonic voice said about unforgiveness.

We asked her, "Is there anyone that you know you can't forgive?"

She quickly replied, "Oh, Yes. There are three people. They hurt me so much that I will never forgive them."

We encouraged her to share the names. She didn't want to tell us, but eventually Suzanne revealed not only the names, but also the evil acts they had done to her. The names matched up with the three names that Old Dad had listed.

For the next two hours we ministered to Suzanne sharing with her that forgiveness was necessary for her to receive Jesus Christ and to have these spirits removed, but she kept resisting. We kept pressing it because forgiveness toward others is imperative for freedom from the bondage of demonic holds.

Suzanne knew she could say the words, but her feelings were so deep that she felt she could not be sincere. Words are so powerful in our lives that even in the most difficult times we can say the right words because we know God approves of what we are saying. This allows the Holy Spirit, as a result of hearing the words come out of one's mouth, to make a clean sweep and change the emotions within us that we knew we couldn't change.

Finally, she said, "Oh, all right. I'll say it. But I don't feel it."

"Just let the words come out of your mouth," we responded. "Let Jesus take care of the feelings."

She named the three people and the evil things they had done, and deliberately stated her forgiveness for their evil actions. Although she did not feel it, God honored her statement of forgiveness.

Then we said, "In the name of Jesus, we want to talk to Old Dad again. Old Dad, are you there?"

He was, "I never thought I would ever hear her say it. She actually forgave those people."

"Now your hold is broken. You have no legal right to torment Suzanne. Is there any reason why you can't leave now?"

He had no other hold. The forgiveness was complete. The demonic hold of these three spirits was broken. It was time to cast them out.

We took authority over the three evil spirits. In the name of Jesus, we commanded them to leave. They left easily because they had no further legal right to stay.

Suzanne's own personality returned with a new found freedom. We recounted briefly what had happened. She only remembered forgiving the three people involved.

We could not let the opportunity pass to ask her again, "Suzanne, would you like to receive the LORD Jesus Christ as your personal Savior now?"

This time she quickly responded, "Oh, Yes!"

I pulled out a copy of the Four Spiritual Laws and went through them with her. We made sure she understood and desired to invite Jesus Christ into her life. I then led her in a prayer of invitation for Jesus to be her LORD and Savior. She now was born again.

It was an exciting afternoon. From that time on, the Christian nurse became a strong co-worker with us in the deliverance ministry.

We had innumerable sessions with Suzanne in the next year. There were other demons that the LORD Jesus scheduled in an orderly fashion to lift from her life. Each of these additional demons had a voice and different personality of its own.

This young lady was very small in stature. Yet in every encounter with each new evil spirit plaguing her, it took five of us to hold her down so that she would not hurt herself or the deliverance workers.

Five of us worked together for over a year, the youth pastor, the nurse and her husband, my wife and myself. We were not experts and had very limited experience, but the youth pastor and I began reading many books about deliverance.

As we ministered to more people and continued to work with Suzanne, some things started to become clear. For example, we learned it doesn't help to try to get rid of all the demons in an individual at one time. They usually needed to go LITTLE BY LITTLE.

"Little by little I will drive them out from before you, until you have increased, and you inherit the land."   *Exodus 23:30*

We also learned demons can still invade and live in Christians. It is just like Apostle Paul stated in Romans 7:15-25. We find ourselves doing things like he did when he said:

"For what I am doing, I do not understand. For what I will to do, that I do not practice; but what I hate, that I do. If, then, I do what I will not to do, I agree with the law that it is good. But now, it is no longer I who do it, but sin that dwells in me. For I know that in me, (that is, in my flesh) nothing good dwells; for to will is present with me, but how to perform what is good I do not find. For the good that I will do, I do not do; but the evil I will not to do, that I practice. Now if I do what I will not to do, it is no longer I who do it, but sin that dwells in me. I find then a law, that evil is present with me, the one who wills to do good. For I delight in the law of God, according to the inward man. But I see another law in my members, warring against the law of my mind, and bringing me into captivity to the law of sin, which is in my members. O wretched man that I am! Who will deliver me from this body of death? I thank God - through Jesus Christ our LORD! So then, with the mind I myself serve the law of God, but with the flesh the law of sin." *Romans 7:15-25*

I believe that the Apostle Paul is talking about demons in much of Romans 7 (Sin you can't control living in born again Christians). We saw evidence of this many times in Suzanne, who had been heavily involved in witchcraft.

Before I explain more and tell you the story of a special prison inmate, I need to let you in on how God opened our eyes to ANGELIC PROTECTION.

In review:

- Christians can be invaded by demons, but not possessed.
- Forgiving others quickly avoids torment.
- Sometimes the voices we hear are real, not hallucinations.

- Satan wants to keep us from coming to Jesus.
- No matter what the enemy says to us, God has the last Word.

There is nothing like freedom.

3

Depend On God For Angelic Protection

By Armour

One of the most valuable lessons we have learned since those first encounters is how to physically control the situation. Our first several situations were very violent.

In working with people up to this point, we would come across some very aggressive demons. Some were so strong that when they took over the body of a Christian, they were able to break or destroy several items in the places where we would meet.

In order to physically protect ourselves, and the counselee from injury, we would use physical force to literally **hold on** to the person we prayed with.

There were usually five of us working together – one person on each limb and one holding the head. After a deliverance session we were all exhausted.

One afternoon my wife and I were sitting at the dining room table reading when the phone rang.   It was a call from a young couple in a neighboring community.

They were crying out for help for a 19 year-old Christian friend who was staying in their home.   They shared with me their story.

This young man, Tyler, had just become a Christian two weeks earlier. He had been living in this Christian home for a short time. Earlier in the day he had gone to the store with the father of this family and wanted to buy a Rock Album. The father advised him not to purchase it, as it would not be honoring to the LORD.

Tyler ignored the counsel and bought the album anyway. As he walked into the Christian home with his new purchase, he went berserk. He became violent with supernatural strength.

Tyler jumped into the family car and attempted to run down the father. He found a huge stump of an old tree, picked it up and threw it on the hood and windshield of the car. It flattened the windshield and hood.

The police were called. They witnessed the acts of violence and wanted to have the young man institutionalized. The police estimated the weight of the tree stump to be at least three hundred pounds.

The couple did not want Tyler in jail. They had taken him in as a ministry and wanted to find help for him. They believed that the violence had been the work of satanic spirits and they called us for help. They asked, "What would you do?"

We remembered the verse "Greater is He that is in you than he that is in the world," and asked for directions to their home. We called the youth pastor but he was not available, so we prayed for wisdom and were on the road in half an hour.

As we came to the country home where they lived, Tyler greeted us in the driveway. There was no sign of violence now. He could remember what he had done, but he had been powerless to stop it.

We went inside and discussed the day's events with the family. We talked of ways that satanic spirits get stirred up, like bringing the rock album into the house. We talked about what it meant to "cleanse your house." They all responded by wanting to get rid of things they knew should not be a part of a Christian's home and began gathering items into the living room they felt should be burned.

We spent about two hours there that afternoon and had a good bonfire in their driveway. At that time, we didn't know how to stir up the demon to show itself. So we prayed together and decided to drive the thirty miles back to our home. We asked them to call us if he became violent again.

They replied, "Can you come back tonight if we call? We feel this evil spirit is not going to be quiet for very long."

We assured them we were only a half-hour away and would be glad to return that evening if the boy became violent again. It was about an hour after we were home when the second call came.

This time we picked up the youth pastor and took him with us. As we drove to their home we filled the youth pastor in on the details, and we prayed together for Tyler and his new found family.

When we arrived, Tyler was still under control and non-violent. He showed the youth pastor the damaged car and the tree stump he could no longer begin to lift in his own strength.

We went inside and began to read scripture together and pray. While we were in the middle of praying, Tyler began to breathe heavily. After a few deep breaths, he suddenly bolted from the chair and ran from the room. He ran out the door and down the road. It had just turned dark.

"What do we do now?" the mother asked.

I went to the door and commanded softly, "Satan, in the name of Jesus, we command you to bring that boy back in here so we can pray with him."

We had learned that we could get some unusual responses when we took authority over Satan and over the demons, but we saw no quick response to that command.

Then I heard my wife praying from the center of the living room a different prayer than I had ever heard before.

"Dear Heavenly Father, the demons in this boy are strong enough that they could wipe out everyone in this room. I am asking that you send your angels to hold on to him. We ask in Jesus name that you send an angel to hold on to each arm and an angel to hold on to each leg. We pray that your angels will bring him back into this room and that they will set him down in the only space left on the sofa. Once he is sitting down that he will be fastened to that particular spot unable to run away again. In Jesus name, Amen!"

We all sat down and waited. We could hear thrashing outside as he was running in the swamp area behind the house. We were all quiet not knowing what to expect. Everything about the evening was new to us. The LORD had us in training.

Then we heard a shuffle at the screen door. I looked up and the boy was standing there. I saw that his eyes were closed. I opened the door and with his eyes closed, he walked around the maze of furniture to the only empty spot on the sofa. He sat down right between the youth pastor and me.

As soon as he was seated, we began declaring war on the demon and commanded it to identify itself. It was the spirit that gave Tyler the supernatural strength to accomplish the feats he had done that afternoon.

A series of demons followed – "Strength," "Destroyer," and "Doubt and Deception." It was quite a battle to force these spirits to surrender one by one. But when their power was diffused and broken, we took authority and commanded the head honcho to tell us if it was a partial or whole demon? A mentor advised us that the next time we had a demon at attention, we should command an answer to this question. Not having done this before, we ordered in Jesus name, and before the throne of the true and living God, that the truth be told whether he was whole or not. To our surprise he said, "I am partial."

We commanded before the throne of the true and living God that he be required to tell the truth. My wife ordered the spirit to tell her in Jesus name, where the other parts were. There was silence for a moment and a low guttural voice answered, "The other parts are with the children in the bedroom." My wife then ordered this spirit to be made whole, and to report to her when it was whole.

We didn't have to wait long until it said "We are all here."

I then proceeded to order them to leave in their entirety, to cancel all past, present and future plans to divide and separate and to go where Jesus sends them, now.

Tyler's personality had been blocked during this encounter. When these spirits were gone, he remembered nothing of what he had said or what the demons had done with his body.

As we sat together on the sofa, we praised God for what He had done, and Tyler was himself again. It looked like our work for that evening was done and we were ready to go home.

As we headed for the front door Tyler said, "Before you go, can anyone tell me why I can't move my hands or feet?" Most of us were taken off guard by that question. We had heard my wife's prayer. We had seen the answer very clearly.

"Do you mean you can't move your hands or feet?"

He said, "I'm completely held down."

I had to check this out and went to the sofa and tried to lift one of his legs, but they were supernaturally fastened.

We came back into the room and my wife prayed, "Thank you Heavenly Father for answering our prayers for protection and for sending angels to bring Tyler inside with an angel on each arm and on each leg just as we asked. I am sorry for forgetting what you had done. We ask you now, in Jesus name to release

Tyler. Thank you for the angelic protection you gave us, in Jesus name, Amen!"

Immediately his hands and feet were free. Tyler began to rub his wrists and ankles with his hands. I asked him to tell us what it felt like to him.

He said, "It was really strange. It felt like someone's hand was wrapped around each of my wrists. It felt like hands were around each ankle. It felt like someone's butt was right in my lap and I couldn't move."

After this experience with Tyler and this family, we never had to have a team ready to hold down the person we were praying for. This took place in 1979, and since then we have had very calm, non–violent sessions. The demons resisted verbally, but not in violent form. The Holy Spirit continued to teach us strategies to aid us in future deliverance sessions.

Our sessions now are very orderly. The violence we had known in the past is no longer characteristic of our ministry. Our voices are calm, the orders are firm and we understand our authority. There is no reason for yelling or screaming, and only one person needs to be in charge. There is much power in the Sword of the Spirit, which is the Word of God. We are now aware there is an earthly army and a heavenly army, and we are privileged to be laboring together with God.

In review:

- Items that belong to Satan's camp should be burned and not kept in our homes.
- Demons can split.
- Most demons have names that describe their assignment.
- Angels can assist us when we ask our Heavenly Father specifically for help.
- We don't have to be afraid. There are unlimited resources from heaven available to assist us.

There is nothing like freedom.

4

Encounters In The Visiting Room

By Armour

Our interest in helping prisoners began when we led a prisoner's wife to the LORD.

We saw a picture on the mantle in her home of her husband in motorcycle gang attire. We inquired who it was and she said, "That's my husband. He's in the State Prison. I go to visit him about every other week."

We encouraged her to tell her husband what had happened to her in receiving Jesus Christ as her Savior. She was a little shook up at the idea, but promised that she would try, if the opportunity came up.

She went down to see him about a week later. And sure enough, God opened the door wide and she stepped through. They had hardly greeted each other when Dan asked, "What happened to you?"

She replied, "I received Jesus as my Savior."

"You what? I can't believe it."

And for the next several minutes he went into a tirade putting down Jesus, God, her, and everything else he could think of. But she calmly faced him and gave a strong testimony of the difference it had made in her life. Then she left and drove back home.

Both she and her husband knew our friend the Christian nurse. So as soon as his wife had left the prison this inmate made a collect call to the nurse at her home.

With hardly a greeting, he demanded, "What happened to my wife?"

The nurse replied, "She received Jesus Christ as her Savior."

"That's what she said. But what happened to her?"

"That is what happened. Could you tell a difference?"

"Well, I don't understand what happened to her. But whatever it is, I want it."

The nurse said, "I'll get in touch with your Chaplain and have him come and see you. He can explain it to you."

"No! You know what she did. Tell me. And whatever she did I'll do it right over the phone!"

So the nurse took her Bible and over the phone she began to explain to this man in prison what it meant to receive Jesus Christ as his Savior. After a few minutes she said, "Dan, would you like to receive Jesus Christ too?"

He was in the hallway of the prison dorm unit during a break after lunch. The hallway was crowded with many of his fellow inmates. When the nurse asked him if he wanted to receive Jesus Christ as his LORD and Savior, Dan tried to say, "No!" But he was shocked when out of his mouth came a humble, "Yes, Yes!"

Right then Dan's knees buckled under him and he felt a heavy weight on his shoulders. He burst into tears as our friend led him to Jesus in front of the other inmates. He later described to us that he felt two strong, heavy hands on his shoulders pushing him to his knees.

His wife went back to see him the next week. She said Dan wanted to meet us, so the following week we drove her to the prison and learned the routine for visiting prisoners.

This was the beginning of a year of almost daily follow up with this man who was incarcerated in a prison miles from our home.

My wife and I were still involved in education at this time. So there were many collect phone calls from Dan in the evenings. Sometimes we would communicate on Saturdays and Sundays as well to help this inmate become established in the Word of God.

However, it soon became apparent that we would need to spend more one on one time with Dan and although it was sort of unusual, there was no better place in the prison to do deliverance counseling than in the visiting room, with guards watching our every move.

There was a Chaplain's office in the school building, but that was basically a desk behind a six-foot clear plastic partition. That wouldn't do.

There were four other offices in the same room but were occupied by the Social Worker, the Psychologist, and the Prisoner Services Director. People were constantly coming and going; every word spoken could be heard by all the other occupants.

The normal actions of a Christian under demonic control are frequently unpredictable, not necessarily violent, but still unpredictable.

We knew it was best to have as much privacy as possibly. So we opted for the most private location we could find – the visiting room.

The visiting room had an acoustic ceiling and carpeted floor that muffled a lot of sounds. In this thirty by thirty foot room, you could be sitting next to another inmate with his family and little children. We were seated in rows, often with people in front and behind us. It seems unbelievable but we could talk in soft tones and no one was aware of our conversation.

We had several dramatic encounters in the visiting room over the years. In our initial dealings with Dan we quickly recognized he had a high I.Q. and what appeared to be a photographic memory. He could read material quickly and retain what he had read. Every time we visited him he shared more findings from his Bible. He was an avid reader and had read through the Bible over thirty times during a two-year period.

Before Dan became a Christian he had an unusual background. He had been adopted into an evil family as a young boy, eventually growing up to work as a college professor, but even then he led what seemed to be multiple lives. He was a professor in the daytime, a member of a motorcycle gang in the evening, and a high priest in the occult at night. He was in prison for running drugs across the state lines.

Dan was familiar with demons and had been utilizing them regularly in the leadership of a church of Satan. There were many demons that had to be cast out one by one. During that first year, we spent many hours in the visiting room, sometimes 9:00 a.m. to 9:00 p.m. on a Saturday.

Frequently, Dan had very little memory of our having been there. He was often taken over by a spirit and it was cast out. As soon as we would command one out another would come to the front. There were some days when we commanded many demons to leave, and other days when one particular spirit would take three to four hours to expel.

It was in the visiting room where we put into practice what we had learned in our other deliverance sessions. With people around us we relied on God's angelic support to not only keep Dan restrained but to keep the voices to almost a whisper.

God's power was amazing as we spent day after day in that small room. The other inmates and their families just a few feet away never realized the person next to them was truly being set free.

On another occasion, while I was still an elementary principal, I received a call from our youth pastor to go to the prison. When we arrived, we prayed before entering the visiting room and asked God to send angels to hold this prisoner down, and keep him under control as he came from his cell to where we were.

As we began our deliverance session, we commanded the demon to speak and tell his name, in the name of Jesus. And he did.

We commanded in the name of Jesus that the demon keep his voice subdued so it would not disturb the guards or any other inmates and visitors in the visiting room. And he did.

It was easy to see that the inmate was struggling.

He fought to get free from the angelic hold. There was an intense battle going on as he resisted the angels.

His right wrist was being held to his right knee by an angel and His left wrist was fastened to his left knee. With the exception of his fingers, he was basically immobile. Still he struggled to get free and attempted to make occult symbols with his fingers.

He looked up to the ceiling of the room and muttered under his breath,

"Be Gone! Be Gone!" I sensed that he was seeing the angels that were in the room.

I said, "No God, please have your angels stay right there. If we need more reinforcements please have them ready."

We ministered to him for about an hour, casting out several demons that named themselves. But one seemed to be giving a special problem.

I was seated to the inmate's right and the youth pastor was on his left. Suddenly the right hand of the inmate slipped from the angel's grip, and the arm swung in an arc hitting me squarely in the nose. My nose began to bleed.

As I grabbed a handkerchief from my pocket to stop the flow of blood on the carpet, I quickly prayed,

"God, send your angelic reinforcements fast. Hold him down so he can't move."

Immediately Dan's free right hand came up on his knee and shot around his left side, and he was held there as if he were in a straight jacket.

It seemed as if a strong angel had come from behind and grabbed his right hand with one hand and his left hand with the other and jerked. I have never seen an angel visibly, but boy is it ever fun to watch them work.

The inmate stayed in this position for about fifteen or twenty seconds, then slowly his left hand returned to his left knee and his right arm went back down to his right knee. He was again held fast.

The resistance was squelched for this demon. And he reluctantly left as we commanded him to, "Go where Jesus sends you". And we were on our way home again.

We learned a lot about different kinds of demons, their roles, and their strengths during our time in the prison visiting room.

Eventually, my wife and I left our jobs in Education and took up the role of Protestant Chaplains in the same prison. We worked for six years as Chaplains daily utilizing the skills the Holy Spirit taught us.

In many of our visits with individual prisoners, we had to deal with demonic manifestations. Without continued angelic help, we would have had violent outbreaks in the visiting room with guards watching our every move. But with this prayer backing, we could minister deliverance in a calm setting as guards watch.

In review:

- God's heart is to set captives free.
- You can win a battle for the LORD in any setting.
- Pray for God to send angelic support.
- Angels are strong and surround us with help.
- Most of the time we do not see angels.
- Pray for physical restraint and voice control.
- Demons must submit before the LORD Jesus Christ.
- God backs us up when we face unusual situations.

There is nothing like freedom.

5

Deliverance By Phone

By Siola

God's power is not limited by distance. When we began to pray for God to cleanse a house from evil spirits, we would pray over one room at a time working our way through the home. Slowly our faith would begin to grow, as we trusted the LORD to come and assist us in battle no matter how far away we were.

As we observed God's power at work, we would pray for God to cleanse the school and the playground where I taught in the name and the blood of Jesus. We would bind up the evil spirits and place the bloodline of Jesus around the property line of the school. We would ask our Heavenly Father to send angels to scrub the floors, walls, ceilings, windows, corners and cracks with the blood of Jesus. We took authority over demons and commanded the invisible forces to be made whole, to cancel all   past, present and future plans to divide and separate, and to go where Jesus Christ sends them. God would answer our prayers even if we prayed from a different location.

Numerous times we would receive a "collect" call from an inmate being harassed by the enemy. It was a privilege to see that God had a way to reach people right where they were even if we could not be. It was impossible to be at the prison twenty-four hours a day, but the ministry could continue by phone.

Prior chapters described battles we fought against the enemy, the authority we have over the enemy, and the fact that Satan and his cohorts must submit to the LORD Jesus Christ. Our faith grows when we see the LORD is greater than we ever imagined and that He is ready to do unusual miracles. James 1 tells us not to waiver back and forth, one day believing God's Word and the next day questioning it.

We need to grasp the truth from the Word of God and believe it with all our heart. Then we will see signs that follow those who believe (Mark 16). God meant what He said, He is faithful and true, and He can be trusted. The power of God has not diminished at all. Instead it can be experienced and demonstrated.

Often I would battle over the phone on behalf of an inmate, taking authority over the spirit the LORD caused to manifest. As the inmate's voice changed, I began dealing with the spirit using the Word to tear its power down. From prison, the inmates call collect and they would take turns making calls, so if the call ended, it was impossible for me to reconnect.

One day as I was ministering to a young man, I could hear the anger of the spirit on the other end of the line. The demon was threatening me to get off the phone or he was going to end it. All of a sudden I heard a dial tone and the call was over.

I was unable to finish helping set this young man free. When I spoke with him later that week, he said he had the receiver up to his ear, but the demon had used his free hand to hang up the phone.

I have always believed God provides a way where there seems to be a dead end. I look for God to show up and if I wait for Him, He always has a plan. So the LORD prompted me the next time I was battling on behalf of someone who called from prison to pray at the beginning, "Father, cover this man with the blood of Jesus, fasten his mouth to the mouthpiece of the phone, fasten his ear to the earpiece, and have an angel hold his free hand so he cannot hang up." Well, it worked! It worked so well that the inmate had to remind me at the end of the call to ask God to release the angels from their holding assignment. It may be hard to believe, but God is able to hear and answer our requests.

There was one time when I forgot to do this while speaking to a woman on the phone. I had been ministering with her and was able to cast out numerous demons. But when I finished commanding the demons to leave, I forgot to pray for God to direct the angels to release her and I hung up the phone. However, the lady was unable to hang up the phone and remained fastened to it.

After about twenty minutes, I realized what I had done and called the woman back. I just got a busy signal because the other end was still off the hook. I tried several times before finally getting through.

I asked the woman if she was still fastened to the phone and she said yes.

When I asked how the call got through, she said her feet were not held down by angels so she was able to hold the line button down with her toe until I called back.

After I prayed for God to have the angels release her, she had complete freedom again. This was the last time we had any trouble remembering to pray for the release of a Christian counselee over the phone.

We have ministered to Christians in this manner for a number of years and we still receive collect calls from prisoners needing release from demonic bondage. But never again did we experience disconnected calls after the LORD showed us how to pray.

In review:

- God has no limits as to what He can do.
- Angels are responsive to God's orders.
- Our warfare prayers are effective even over long distances.
- Stretch your faith and it will keep increasing.
- Faith is necessary to please the LORD, He will bring answers to our requests.

There is nothing like freedom.

"This is the **blood** of the covenant, which is poured out for many for the forgiveness of sins." *Matthew 26:28*

"In Him we have redemption through His **blood,** the forgiveness of sins, in accordance with the riches of God's grace." *Ephesians 1:7*

"He did not enter by means of the blood of goats and calves; but he entered the Most Holy Place once for all by His own **blood,** having obtained eternal redemption." *Hebrews 9:12*

"For you know that it is not with perishable things such as silver and gold that you were redeemed from the empty way of life handed down to you from your forefathers, but with the precious **blood of Christ**, a lamb without blemish or defect." *I Peter 1:18, 19*

"In Fact, the law requires that nearly everything be **cleansed with blood**, and without the shedding of blood there is no forgiveness."
Hebrews 9:22

"But if we walk in the light, as he is in the light, we have fellowship with one another, and the **blood of Jesus**, his Son, purifies us from all sin."
1John 1:7

"…and from Jesus Christ, who is the faithful witness, the firstborn from the dead, and the ruler of the kings of the earth. To him who loves us and has freed us from our sins by his **blood**." *Revelation 1:5*

"They overcame him by the **blood of the Lamb** and by the word of their testimony." *Revelation 12:11a*

"He is dressed in a robe dipped in **blood**." *Revelation 19:13a*

6

The Blood Of Jesus

By Siola

The importance of the blood of Jesus can never be overemphasized. The perfect blood of Jesus comes from our Heavenly Father. The blood that Jesus shed on the cross is pure and holy, while our blood is stained and polluted with the sins of our fathers and the imperfection of our own lives.

Some groups are turned off at the mention of blood. There are denominations determined to remove all references to the blood of Jesus from the hymnal because it may be offensive to those who come to worship with them. I love the song that says, "There is power, power, wonder working power, in the blood of the Lamb; there is power, power, wonder working power, in the precious blood of the Lamb."

When Moses was assigned by God to be Israel's deliverer, he was to bring the children of Israel out from the grip of Pharaoh in Egypt. The first-born of an unbelieving family was doomed to die. In order to be protected from death, Moses gave the children of Israel one last instruction. They were to spread the fresh blood of a young lamb on the sides and top of the doorway to their homes. When the angel of death saw the blood, it passed over the home.

The lamb was representative of the future Lamb, our LORD Jesus Christ who would someday spill his perfect blood on the cross so that your sins and mine would be forgiven, guaranteeing our rescue from eternal death and assurance of eternal life.

The Blood of Jesus at an Abortion Clinic

A young man I have known for years shared an experience he and his girlfriend had at an abortion clinic. His girlfriend found herself pregnant with his child and insisted she was going to have the baby aborted. He urged her to reconsider her decision. She was intent with ending the pregnancy and decided to visit an abortion clinic, which in turn tested her and verified her pregnancy. A date and time was scheduled for her to return to have the procedure done.

The young man continued his plea to save the child, but the mother had her heart closed to even consider sparing the baby's life. Though the father was strongly against the decision to abort the child, he opted to support her by accompanying her to the clinic that day and to comfort her after the surgery. They arrived at the clinic on time but had to wait until her name was called. The young man's heart was broken as he thought of the baby he had fathered. The child's life would be ended in a short time. He reached over and laid his hand on his girlfriend's abdomen and prayed to God silently.

He asked God to cover the baby with the blood of Jesus and confessed the sin that was about to take place.

An attendant came into the waiting area, called his girlfriend's name and ushered her into a room. They set up the ultra sound machine to locate the fetus in the womb. The doctor searched over and over with the machine but the staff could not find an embryo to be aborted. The doctor refused to follow through with the abortion even though the young woman urged him to go ahead based on the previous test showing evidence of life.

The abortion was unable to be performed that day. The blood of Jesus was so powerful that the baby was hidden and protected. Although the baby was eventually lost to a miscarriage months later, God gave a miraculous answer to a father's urgent prayer.

The Blood of Jesus Protects on Vacation

My husband and I chose to celebrate our 42nd wedding anniversary by staying in a trailer at a State Park on Lake Michigan. On the second night I could see a storm coming over the lake heading our direction. As we waited for a signal to see if we needed to leave and head for the safety of our home, we prayed and asked God to cover us with the blood of Jesus and all those in its path. The wind increased in velocity to one hundred and thirty miles an hour. It was not wise to consider driving home. Debris was flying everywhere, branches were snapping, and trees were being uprooted. Fire trucks and ambulances were running about. It was like a war zone.

Our trailer did not move or shake even when we sensed that the strongest part of the storm was over our heads.

When the storm was over and I went outside, a passerby handed me a block of wood and asked if it belonged to us. It did. As soon as the owner of the trailer came by to assess the damage, he was amazed the trailer was still standing since the block of wood should have been supporting the hitch and keeping the trailer in balance. There was nothing to hold the trailer upright, it should have toppled over along with the others in the park.

In the calm after the storm, we saw around us thirty-six recreational vehicles that had been demolished. The majority were motor homes, a number of trailers, and a few pop-up campers. They were flipped on their sides breaking cabinets, furniture, dishes, and windshields. Side panels were dented and ruined.

God specifically intervened that night and no one in the area was killed or severely injured. Through it all, the trailer did not sustain a single dent or broken window. We were completely cocooned in His protection, and escaped unharmed. A wonderful anniversary present.

Voices in the Night

One night a young lady we knew returned home to her apartment and as she pulled into the driveway she heard angry voices. Amber looked for the people who were arguing and screaming at each other, but she couldn't find anyone so she entered her home. Once inside Amber still heard the vicious voices. She searched the apartment but there was no one there. As the evening progressed, she still continued to hear voices.

At eleven o'clock that night, the phone rang and it was Amber. "Armour and Siola, something strange is going on. I can hear a group of people screaming at each other, but when I searched the driveway and the inside of my apartment, there is no one. I have my Bible open. Will you come over and pray?"

My husband and I changed clothes, grabbed a few things and arrived at Amber's in fifteen minutes. It was a two-story house located in a college community and she lived on the top floor.

We evaluated the situation and determined a demonic influence or evil spirit resided in the home. It has been our experience that if certain occult rituals have been practiced previously in a location, the evil spirits have freedom to claim the territory as their own. It gives the evil spirits a legal right to abide there.

Some disturbances we have dealt with are: tapping sounds, objects that move by themselves, feeling touches while one sleeps, glimpses of moving shadows, heavy oppression in the air, a smell of sulfur, nothing seems to go right, or even a dark and oppressive cloud that doesn't go away. In one home where we ministered, the evil spirits had affected the furnace and the home was icy cold. Once the spirits were commanded out, the furnace began to work again.

The couple living below Amber joined us and agreed that since they moved to this home sounds and tapping could be heard upstairs. The five of us worked as a team and went from room to room praying and taking authority over these entities in Jesus' name. We confessed the sins of the previous tenants and commanded the spirits lingering in the house to leave in their entirety and to go where Jesus sends them.

Every room of the house was prayed over, so we headed to the basement. We found the basement to be damp and dingy with an unfinished area of cement block walls. One room was more oppressive than the others. This room had no windows, but it contained an altar. It was a dungeon. We confessed the sins and abominations that had occurred in the room. As soon as we took authority over the invisible spirits and cast them out in Jesus name, the oppression was lifted.

The angels had removed all the invisible evil forces and the house was free from the symptoms of demonic activity. Those living in the home did not experience any further disturbances.

The gift Satan gives to those he wants to control is fear. The gift that God gives is faith.

"For God has not given us the spirit of fear, but of power and of love and of a sound mind."
2 Timothy 1:7

"The LORD is my light and my salvation; Whom shall I fear? The LORD is the strength of my life; Of whom shall I be afraid?" *Psalm 27:1*

When séances are held, witchcraft rituals practiced, demons conjured up, spells cast on people, the drinking blood of animals or humans, sacrificing to Satan, etc., it gives a legal right for demons to saturate the area where these sessions are held and consider it their home. They have freedom to perform evil. Satan also gives the spirits instructions to affect the lives of those participating.

This legal right can be easily taken away by talking to God about what is going on. A Christian takes authority quickly by stating, "I bind you in the name of Jesus, and I command you to leave our presence and to go where Jesus is sending you." We then watch the LORD JESUS and His angels arrest the spirits and remove them faster than you can imagine.

"But Jesus looked at [them] and said, 'With men this is impossible, but with God all things are possible.'" *Matthew 19:26*

At your first encounter, it may sound eerie or morbid and the first inclination is to walk away or run and never choose to hear about the darkness again. But when you are aware all of heaven is behind you as you step forward against the enemy, and realize your family or friends can be set free, you become exhilarated to be involved in the process.

We have found that using the name of Jesus and the blood of Jesus over a location is amazing and it has the power to break all witchcraft curses that have been placed on an area. There is nothing like the name of Jesus and the blood of Jesus, for it has the ability to bring heaven down to stamp out Satan's plans. Angels come with chains and arrest the demonic teams. You don't have to do it. Jesus does it all. He brings all evil to a screeching halt, and

Satan's plans are destroyed, immobilized, and removed, never to return. How cool is that?

Today we have a practical way of applying the blood of Jesus to our homes and families. In our years of experiencing God's protection, we ask God frequently for the covering of the blood of Jesus. We have included in the next section prayers to assist you in your daily growth with the LORD. As you battle in prayer you will find great protection against the enemy. It is hard to be a soldier in God's army and not know how to actively participate in the fight.

I know that I do not want to be in the back row of a battalion. I want to be in the front row, moving out in the offensive, commanding Satan out of my way because I am coming through in the name of Jesus. Sometimes I see Christians who have not been taught to fight. They are still God's children, but you might find them in a back corner, licking their wounds because they are hurt and bleeding. They have become preoccupied with their injuries and have been distracted from fighting the enemy and his forces. Jesus set the example and we are safe following his pattern.

Satan's plan is to have you focus on yourself so you are unable to land your blows in the enemy camp. As a result, you end up not involved in the teamwork necessary to ask God to send angels to push back the forces of hell – to the north, south, east, and west. We can ask our heavenly Father to send the angel of the LORD, to come with his sword dipped in the blood of Jesus, to carve a way for us to get through to victory. Amen!

You will find in the following pages how the Holy Spirit taught us to pray when we knew nothing about warfare. These are solid, practical prayers that have proven successful in many battles over the years. Use them in praying for yourself, your family, and your friends. Frequently learn to spiritually cleanse your home, church, work place, and school.

Develop confidence as a soldier of Jesus Christ. This will eliminate fear when it comes to demonic forces that come against you and your loved ones. Understand the authority the LORD Jesus has given you and observe the protection of the blood of Jesus in your everyday living. We pray you are encouraged and inspired by the stories you read.

Take your position on the battlefield with courage and strength. God has given you a high position in his army when you put yourself through His boot camp. You are "more than a conqueror." As you develop strategies and discipline in God's army through the tools in this book, you will move out in the offensive, you will taste the victory, and you will notice the change that has occurred in your life as a result.

Spiritual Warfare Prayer

Abba Father,

I bow down and worship you. I am thankful that you are my Father. You are a good Father. Cover me with Jesus' blood for my protection right now. Thank you for sending Jesus to die in my place. You have forgiven all of my sins. You have adopted me into your family. You have given me eternal life. Open my eyes so that I may see you working all around me. Because of Jesus, Satan and all evil spirits are under my feet. Satan, I command you to move out of my way, in Jesus name, and go where Jesus sends you. I bring the blood of Jesus between us.

Thank you for the pieces of Armor that I will now put on. The Helmet of Salvation to protect my mind. The Breastplate of Righteousness protects my breathing and my heart. I buckle the Belt of Truth because you hate lies. I put on the Sandals of Peace, so that I can be a peacemaker. I raise the Shield of Faith up high so that Satan's arrows will not land on me. I take the Sword of the Spirit (the Word of God) and pierce Satan every time I use it.

I reject all the lies and bad ideas Satan would put into my mind. I choose to obey you. Show me the things that I am doing that do not please you. I choose to quickly forgive those who have hurt me. I put away selfishness and put on love. I put away fear and put on courage. I put away the strong desire to want things and I put on purity, honesty and doing the right things. If I have any idols I worship more than you, help me get rid of them. I want to do your will as your Word has shown me.

Thank you for sending so many blessings from heaven upon me. I give myself to you as a living sacrifice. I pray in Jesus' name with thanksgiving. Amen

Spiritually Cleansing Your Home

Prayer,

I place the blood of Jesus on the property line of our home and on the doorposts of my house.

I bind up the spirits in the atmosphere, under the ground, in the water, and over my home, in Jesus name. I take authority over any evil spirits in the house or in any of the buildings on the property. I bind them up in Jesus name.

I command these spirits to be made whole. I command you to cancel all past, present and future plans to divide and separate. I command you to go where Jesus sends you now.

Heavenly Father, I ask you to send angels with buckets of the blood of Jesus to scrub the walls, floors, ceilings, windows, doors, corners and cracks. Father, please send as many angels as you know that we need right now. Thank you for all the reinforcements that are available to us, in Jesus name, Amen.

I recommend you use the prayer for cleansing your home daily. It will keep your home spiritually clean and full of peace.

I am assured that when I use the term bind that immediately God is sending angels to arrest, wrap in chains, and put these spirits on freeze. Now they are incapable of doing what they have been assigned to do by Satan.

We have found that demons can split. In one case, as we were praying with a young man, the spirit was speaking out through him and we commanded the spirit to tell us whether it was a partial or whole spirit. It stated that it was partial and the other parts were with the children in the bedroom. Since the LORD brought this to our attention and we understood our authority in Jesus, we commanded the spirit to be made whole and to report to us when it was whole. This meant that the other pieces with the children had to join this one and then we could remove it in its entirety from the family, in Jesus name. It is important for you to know that evil spirits have the ability to split into several parts.

Covering Medication

We recommend that a person on medication continue the plan set before them by their doctor. It is not our desire to interfere or to suggest anyone stop taking medication.

We have found the following prayer to be a breakthrough in this area. It provides peace and trust in the LORD. As healing occurs, the doctors will see the change and will begin to cut back the medication or even eliminate it.

Prayer,

In Jesus' name, we pray that the blood of Jesus will surround and cover the medication entirely that has just been taken, anywhere that it is located in _____'s body.

We ask you heavenly Father, to neutralize all the side effects of the medication. We ask heavenly Father that whatever is good in this prescription would be kept and used. But whatever is harmful to _____ would be sealed off with the blood of Jesus and washed out of their body, in Jesus name.

Thank you Jesus, Amen!

Covering Internal Systems

Covering all internal systems of your body with the blood of Jesus provides a great deal of protection. It reduces and relieves pain in some cases and settles anxieties. It will also help one to breathe the breath of God during a difficult time.

The blood of Jesus traps the enemy in areas where one is afflicted and oppressed. It affects the area where there is a stronghold of the enemy.

Prayer,

In the name of Jesus, I ask you heavenly Father to saturate me with the blood of Jesus from the top of my head to the bottom of my feet.

I ask that all internal systems be immersed with the blood of Jesus.

I ask that the blood of Jesus be running in and through my blood system cleansing, trapping, and eliminating toxins and demonic strongholds in the blood that are effecting my health.

I ask you heavenly Father to cover my mind, emotions, and will, conscious, subconscious, unconscious and hidden emotions with the blood of Jesus.

I ask you to cover my senses with the blood of Jesus to saturate my sight, smell, tasting, hearing, and touching. Saturate my lips, teeth, and gums, mouth cavity, tongue, esophagus, voice box and trachea with Jesus' blood.

I ask you to cover the glandular system with the blood of Jesus, the pituitary gland, the hypothalamus gland, the thymus, the lymph glands and lymph nodes, the adrenal and thyroid gland, and the endocrine glands.

I ask you heavenly Father to saturate the respiratory system with the blood of Jesus, saturate the digestive system with the blood of Jesus, and to saturate the reproductive organs with the blood of Jesus.

I ask you heavenly Father to cover the pancreas, the liver, the spleen, the heart, the kidneys, the gall bladder and bladder, and the intestines with the blood of Jesus.

I ask you to saturate the bones, joints and marrow with the blood of Jesus, and to saturate the muscles, tendons and ligaments with the blood of Jesus.

I ask you heavenly Father to cover the circulatory system, the arteries and veins, and the heart with the blood of Jesus, to cover the epidermis and dermis layers with the blood of Jesus, to cover the nervous system with the blood of Jesus, and to cover the immune system with the blood of Jesus. Amen!

Cleansing the House and the Land

"Behold, I give you power to tread on serpents and scorpions, and over all the power of the enemy: and nothing shall by any means hurt you."
Luke 10:19

Prayer,

I put on the armor of God everyday. Father God, please fasten the helmet of salvation, the breastplate of righteousness, the girdle of truth, the sandals of peace, the sword of the spirit, and the shield of faith securely so that not one of the pieces of armor will fall off during the night. I am young and I am strong, in Jesus name. I am a warrior and Jesus makes me stronger every time I meet with warriors young and old. Wherever my feet walk, I take authority over anything under my feet.

I have authority in my feet. I have destiny in my hands. David confidently stated to the giant Goliath before the giant was overcome..."You come to me with a javelin, spear and sword. But I come to you in the name of the LORD my God."

Jesus Christ has already won the victory for you on the cross.

I ask you Heavenly Father to spread and pour the blood of Jesus over the property line. Father, please send angels to drench the atmosphere over this place with the blood of Jesus. I confess any sins committed here in behalf of those living here. I repent of any abomination hidden in the ground causing curses upon this home. I break generational curses because of the sins of the ancestors. I take back the ground that was given to Satan and I give it to you, Heavenly Father. I ask you to lift off the curses from this land, in Jesus name.

If there is blood that cries out to you from the ground in this place, I repent for the loss of life and the sin involved. I ask that the ground would be cleansed with the blood of Jesus, and that curses would be lifted from all effected by this act. I ask for a waterfall of the blood of Jesus to cover this house in and out, and to also place the blood on the doorposts. I bind all evil spirits in the ground, in or on the house, in any room, in or on any of the buildings on the property, in Jesus name. I command you to be made whole. I command you to cancel all past, present and future *plans to divide and separate and that you go where Jesus sends you. Everything that reports to you must do the same. All connected, related, resulting demons, must go where Jesus sends you.*

Please send angels with buckets of the blood of Jesus to scrub the walls, ceilings, floors, windows, doors, corners and cracks. Father, please send as many angels as you know we need right now. Thank you for all the reinforcements that are available to us, in Jesus name. Amen!

In his book, *"Like a Roaring Lion,"* author George Otis tells of a Hollywood home owned by a well-known actor that had been purchased by Christians for use as a house church. The new owners proceeded to have it spiritually cleansed by setting up a large speaker system and loudly playing scripture 24/7 for three weeks before beginning to remodel.

Maybe you have visited a place and suddenly sensed something different around you. This is what is known as "transference of evil spirits." For example, you may be visiting with someone and when you leave you seem to be thinking the same way this individual was while you were with him or her. You know it is not you and you wonder where these thoughts and words came from.

It is a good idea to bind up evil spirits before you have an appointment, a meeting, a lunch engagement, etc. by stating, *"I bind up any spirits that would attempt to interfere, I put you on hold, in Jesus name."* A simple procedure like this limits and chains up predominant spirits in another individual. It gives you freedom to be yourself without demonic control.

You can pray, "*I block any transference of evil spirits of any kind that might try to influence me in any way, in Jesus name.*"

We would also recommend spiritually cleansing a motel room with prayer before using it. Demonic debris left in rooms as a result of the type of films that were viewed, certain activity done in secret, and any unseen spirits that are still there can effect your thinking or your attitude toward things without it being intentional on your part.

In review:

- Become familiar with verses about the Blood.
- The Blood of Jesus is more powerful than we can comprehend. Specifically apply it to your life. Ask God to help you.
- Read Your Personal Warfare Prayer daily.
- Put on the armor of God daily.
- Keep your house spiritually clean.
- Protect your body where the Holy Spirit is housed. Cleanse all parts with the blood of Jesus.
- Cover medication with the blood of Jesus.

There is nothing like freedom.

7

Declaring War Against The Enemy

By Siola

It is vital to the spiritual battle to learn how to take authority over evil spirits in the name of Jesus. The following prayers and commands will enable you to go into the fight prepared to declare war, to inflict punishment, to enter direct combat, and to break curses. There is victory in Jesus!

Declaring War

Prayer,

Heavenly Father, we submit ourselves to you and to the direction of the Holy Spirit as we begin this prayer time. Your word says, "Submit yourselves therefore to God, resist the devil, and he will flee from you." (James 4:7) We are thankful that the battle is the Lord's, so we put it all in your hands now. I ask that you would put on us the full armor of God, fastening all the pieces securely for a full twenty-four hours. Let none of the pieces fall off during our sleep. Help us to hold up the shield of faith.

Severely bind up all spirits of deception and lying, that there may be no interference. I bind up all the strongmen in all our lives. I declare war upon the enemy, in Jesus name. I take authority over you in the heavenlies and here on earth, in Jesus name. Heavenly Father, you know _____ very well, better than anyone.

We believe that you also know where the deliverance should start and when it should end. We put ourselves under the leadership of our LORD Jesus Christ who is the Commander in Chief of the heavenly army and the earthly army. Thank you that we can draw from your unlimited resources.

May we listen to you and choose to be humble through these proceedings for we already know that pride is what caused Satan and his angels to be put out of heaven. I realize that you will not allow this fight against the enemy to be victorious if we think we have the answers and do not inquire of you.

I love you LORD, I depend upon you, and thank you the victory has already been won! Hallelujah!

In Jesus name, Amen!

When in a deliverance session, I believe in asking God to send angels with punishments and surprise attacks on the enemy camp to begin dismantling his barricades. This creates a great advantage and puts us ahead in the battle.

Punishments

I ask Heavenly Father that you would send angels with the following punishments to the enemy camp:

- *999 bazillion – trillion jagged rocks*
- *Avalanches of hailstones*
- *Avalanches of grinding wheels*
- *Avalanches of boulders*
- *Avalanches of fire balls*
- *Earthquakes, rumblings*
- *Lightning, thunder*

Panic, havoc, destruction, pandemonium, chaos, anger, fear, wrath, finger of God, hornets of the Lord, hounds of heaven, curses of the Midianites, Moabites, Ammonites, Edomites, burning judgment, sulfur, confusion, forgetfulness, destruction.

Hot burning coals, hot scalding water, acid, battering rams, branding irons, arrows dipped in the blood of Jesus, heavenly bulldozers, and heavenly steamrollers.

Heavenly Father would you please send all the punishments stated in the Word from Genesis to Revelation, and multiply that times infinity.

I ask for whatever came down upon Sodom and Gomorrah to land upon these teams and let them know we mean business.

At this point, you can use the specific commands for direct combat found below, in Jesus' name. You may experience a physical reaction of some sort and the quoting or reading of scripture by those assisting in the deliverance is powerful.

Commands to use in direct combat

At this point you are no longer praying, but have entered into a specific battle during a deliverance session. The following commands have been very effective:

- ❖ In Jesus' name I command you to be at attention!
- ❖ I command the evil spirit that the LORD Jesus has already chosen to be the spokesman, or first to come up and report!
- ❖ I command you in Jesus name to come into the breathing passage!
- ❖ I command you in Jesus name to speak using _____ faculties!
- ❖ In the name of Jesus, I command you to have a voice to speak and ears to hear!

During deliverance there is only one person assigned to command. The group present must be prayerful and ready to use their swords, which is the Word of God. Confusion or high emotional outbursts are not appropriate and as you will see not necessary. Save your energy. You are not the one battling; God and the angels are battling in the heavenlies where the real war is being fought.

Study Deuteronomy 7 to see why the LORD Jesus wants us to drive them out

Prayer to Break Witchcraft Curses

In the name of Jesus and by the blood of Jesus, I break all hexes, vexes, fetishes, charms, jinx, spells, witchcraft, bewitchments, enchantments, love potions, psychic prayers, sexual curses, wishes, voodoo, black and white magic curses, crystal ball curses, Ouija curses, tarot curses, drug curses, Indian curses. We bind up and cast out all the above, in Jesus name. I bind up New Age Movement curses, Illuminati curses, Council of Thirteen curses, and curses coming from Wicca. I include other occult groups that are sending curses and those who are talking about me. I forgive them but I do no accept the curses. Psalm 109 says, "Let him that loves cursing receive it unto himself."

In the name of Jesus, Amen.

We have shared with you specific warfare prayers we have used for years. These are all tools to help you clear the debris that Satan would put into your life to hinder you and to rob you of the blessings God has for you.

In review:

- Be ready and prepared to declare war.

- The name and the blood of Jesus is more powerful than we can comprehend.
- We have the authority to ask God to send punishments to the enemy.
- God and the angels will battle for you.
- Curses can be broken through Jesus.
- Learn to use the weapons God has provided for you.

There is nothing like freedom.

8

An Amazing God

By Siola

When my husband and I began our chaplaincy at the prison in Michigan we were unsure how we would be received but we enjoyed the contact we had with the young men. Many groups and individuals from colleges throughout the state would assist us over the years along with a number of church ministries. Our son facilitated students from his University to come on a weekly basis to lead Bible Studies, and our daughter would occasionally help with the music. We consistently organized weekly Bible classes, planned plays, dramas, and even invited large churches to come put on concerts. In addition to Armour's preaching, we often conducted three two-hour services on a given Sunday. During the week we filled our free time with individual appointments.

Divine appointments

One particular afternoon, a young man, Randy, was walking from his cell to the gym for a workout. There was no one else on the sidewalk with him at the time, but as he was approaching the gym his body was pushed and turned around back toward the school building. Randy was understandably shocked, but straightened himself out and headed back to the gym.

Again Randy was forcefully pushed and turned around in the direction of the school. Randy fought the unseen force for a second time, still attempting to get to the gym. After the fourth occurrence, he thought he'd better go into the school. He entered the building where the college classes were held and slowly peeked into each classroom. They were all empty until he stuck his head into the room where Armour and I sat alone.

"Hello" he said. "I think this is where I'm supposed to be." He then went on to explain how he was 'led' to meet us and share his story. It was a divine appointment that helped to guide Randy into a wonderful new phase of his life and one we will never forget.

Carol was a young mother with two adorable children. We met many times when demons were afflicting her, and God with his mighty angels, lifted her oppressions. Carol had been dealing with back pain, but one day the pain was so excruciating her family had to take her to the Emergency Room.

After many tests the doctors came to Carol's room and told her that from now on her life would be different. She would not have the use of her legs, she would need to depend on a wheelchair for the rest of her life, and she would not be able to take care of her children. Her bones were deteriorating and she would soon be paralyzed.

Carol's spirit was dashed to the ground with this news. She placed a call to our home and I could hear the brokenness that had come over her from the doctor's diagnosis. I agreed to pray, but wasn't sure deliverance prayer would be appropriate at this time.

I asked Carol, "Are you in a private room?"

She answered, "No, I am sharing it with another person."

There were nurses coming in and out of her room. I shared with Carol that I would not be combating the enemy as usual, but certainly we would pray and wait for God's appointed time. As we were talking, her voice changed and I knew what that meant – the voice I heard was not Carol's. Trying to be wise, I decided I would pray more specifically at another time. I thought surely the LORD doesn't want me to fight the enemy now under these conditions. The spirit kept talking and all of a sudden the call was ended. There was no one on the other end. I called for Carol..."Carol, can you hear me?" No answer.

As I sat in my dining room contemplating what had just occurred, I began to feel the LORD had presented a situation that could have been remedied had I done my part. Everything appeared it was not the time to go into combat as I have many times before. I sulked that I had not prayed, especially after I realized I failed to ask God to fasten the earpiece to Carol's ear, the mouthpiece to her mouth, an angel to hold her other hand to prevent an evil spirit from hanging up.

I confessed to the LORD I did not respond to the call as He desired for me to do, and prayed for another opportunity so I could be faithful in what He had taught me to do. I prayed that Carol would place a call again. I waited all day, but no calls came from the hospital.

Later in the evening the phone rang and I was ready to battle. It was from Carol, but I have never received a call like this in my ministry before. It was not her voice.

The voice on the other end said, "The LORD wants you to know that He is aware of the crushing news that was given to Carol today. He wants you to know that it will not be a reality. She will be well and the LORD has plans to heal her completely. She will not be confined to a wheelchair for the rest of her life."

"The LORD also wants you to know that it was not a demon that cut off the first call today, but it was Michael, God's warrior angel who ended the conversation. The LORD also wants you to know that there are 5,000 angels in her room right now."

Later on that night, barely able to contain myself with the miraculous intervention of God in both Carol's life and mine, I placed a call to her room to see if I could make a connection. Carol answered and she was herself. She did not recall any conversation on the phone, although she did remember placing a call to me.

I was able to pass on the message from the LORD that He wanted me to share with Carol. It was His direct word to her. Today she is not in a wheelchair, she is leading a normal life, and able to care for her children. Carol received healing and deliverance from her Heavenly Father who loves her so much.

That night, she lay in her hospital bed trying to figure out how five thousand angels could squeeze into her room.

Diana has a rifle and is calling for you

A woman who had recently come out of the occult and was receiving deliverance prayer weekly by our warfare team, stopped to visit one of our team member's homes.

Very unexpectedly a different personality emerged. Diana was not herself. She noticed a squirrel rifle propped up in a corner and after snatching it; she headed for a back bedroom of the house. Diana told the team member to get Siola on the phone and ask her to come over.

I received a call from my friend who said, "Diana is here, she is manifesting, she has a rifle in the back bedroom with her and she is calling for you. Siola, can you come over?"

My husband prayed for me before I left.

When I arrived at the door, a voice bellowed from the back of the house saying, "Siola, come back here, I want to see you."

I walked into the living room and sat down. Demons will speak through the vocal cords, and the LORD has helped me to discern when it really is the person or if it is a demonic take over. Through past experiences, I knew I was dealing with an evil spirit. I responded with, "I do not take orders from you, but just the opposite, I take authority over you and I order you to come into the living room and hand over the rifle to me, in Jesus name."

This spirit had no intention to submit, but believed he would take me down.

The verbal battle continued with repeated threats and plans to take my life. After some time we could hear Diana leave the bedroom and walk down the hallway toward the living room.

My position was firm. I wasn't going to give in. Diana arrived at the edge of the living room. She propped up the rifle on a wooden shelf and took aim. The ugly, vile statements of hatred kept coming at me.

Commands, in Jesus name, were repeated. Everything the demon said was an attempt to intimidate and provoke me into feeling fear that something was going to happen. I blocked those words out of my mind and focused on the LORD's strength and the power of His Word. God is not a liar and I can depend on Him. I claimed the victory was mine because of the Word of God. I persisted with the commands and never retreated. I used scripture passages, and in Jesus name gave the spirit orders that he was not in charge and he must hand the rifle over to me.

Diana then stepped into the living room, still aiming the rifle at me, determined to shoot. I never weakened. The LORD Jesus gave me strength and supplied me with faith to persevere.

The evil spirit brought Diana closer and set the rifle flush against my right temple. I commanded again, "Hand over the rifle, in Jesus name!"

Diana dropped the rifle into my hands and the battle ended. She sat down on the sofa, and with the assistance of my prayer partner, we prayed and commanded the demons to submit. Diana was set free that afternoon by the LORD Jesus Himself.

"Behold, I give you the authority to trample on serpents and scorpions, and over **all** of the power of the enemy, **and nothing shall by any means hurt you.**"   *Luke 10:19*

"The **name of the LORD** is a strong tower; The righteous **run into it and are safe.**" *Proverbs 18:10*

Cardiac arrest gone

My friend Sandy was shopping for groceries at the local supermarket when she collapsed and fainted to the floor. An ambulance was called and she was taken to the nearest hospital. They placed Sandy in a room and hooked her up to a number of cardiac testing machines.

After a few hours, Sandy called me at home and shared the details that lead up to her being hospitalized. She asked for prayer and we agreed the LORD would reveal the condition that caused her to faint and that healing would come quickly. I added to the prayer that the spirit of Cardiac Arrest would be bound in Jesus name. I commanded it to be made whole, to cancel all future plans to divide and separate, and to go where Jesus wanted it to go.

As I finished the prayer, Sandy shared what had happened while I prayed. "Siola, as you were praying something was pulled out from the soles of my feet that felt as though it had been fastened to my hips." I thanked her for her observations. She was planning to call me when more of her condition was determined.

By watching God work when freeing a person from an attack, I have observed evil spirits leaving in many ways. They can leave through the air passages: coughing, yawning, sneezing, even lightheadedness. The angels are the ones who remove the demons and in this case they yanked them from her feet.

Back at the nurse's station, the staff noticed the cardiac machines in Sandy's room were now reading normal. A nurse entered Sandy's room and asked, "Have you done anything to the machines? They are no longer showing any abnormal readings? Did you tamper with them in any way?"

My friend told the nurse she had not touched the machines. The nurse wasn't satisfied with her answer, so the door to her room was kept wide open. They continued to watch her closely. After some time, the cardiac machines continued to give normal readings so Sandy was able to go home, free and clear with no physical problems. God delivered her from a heart condition.

A stroke begins to move in on Lana

Lana was stiffening. The muscles on one side of her face were beginning to droop and speaking was difficult. She called my home, but the voice was undistinguishable. I had difficulty hearing the words.

I asked, "Lana is this you? Are you having trouble? Do you want me to come over?" She grunted a response.

I called a friend to meet me at Lana's home. When we arrived, Lana was in the middle of her living room, lying very still in a Lazy-Boy chair. She was unable to speak but she could hear me. I asked her if she would allow me to pray for her. She grunted a yes.

The only thing Lana could do at this point was to place her free hand on the area of her body that needed prayer. I followed her lead.

She started by tapping her lips with three fingers. I began the attack against the enemy affecting her speech. I bound the enemy and cast it out.

Lana tapped the side of her face. I prayed by taking authority over spirits that were hiding in the muscles and nerves in her face. I commanded them to be made whole, to cancel all past, present and future plans to divide and separate, and to go where Jesus sends them.

Lana tapped the top of her arm and we bound up the spirits effecting paralysis on her left side, and cast this team out. The last area Lana tapped were the fingers of her left hand. I bound up the spirit of stroke, taking authority over it and casting it out.

Within moments, Lana arose from the recliner and the more she moved, the perkier she got. She was soon skipping around her kitchen like a young girl. The LORD had healed her completely.

She mentioned she had a doctor's appointment within an hour. We asked, "Would you like us to drive you there?" Lana declined the offer.

"I feel great and I will enjoy driving by myself today."

Before leaving, we prayed for the Holy Spirit to fill in all the gaps where these spirits were being removed and to heal all the areas the enemy wanted to dismantle in Lana's life.

We found where true deliverance takes place, healing also follows. Praise God! Hold your position and persevere. Jesus' name is above every name. Using the name of Jesus breaks the back, the scepter and the rod of the oppressor.

All of this happened so quickly. The two of us who went to Lana's home did not know ahead of time why Lana had called us. We just began to pray and God showed himself strong just as quickly.

Under normal conditions, knowing ahead of time what was happening, we would have called 911 for assistance, but it was definitely a leading of the LORD that went beyond our expectations. We still are amazed as we think of the visit and miraculous work, the glory all goes to God Himself.

"With men this is impossible, but with God all things are possible." *Matthew 19:26b*

Diabetes, no longer a threat!

There are many of you who know someone in your family or circle of friends that is afflicted with a diabetic condition. In some cases, as it was with my husband, it could be traced to his family line. My father-in-law also was diabetic.

In the medical profession there is no cure for this illness. As a result one would not expect this disease to go away. My husband had difficulty controlling his sugar levels and had to give himself an injection of insulin daily.

Once a year, my husband, Armour, and I visited a wonderful little church outside of Chicago. They put on a Spiritual Warfare Conference and brought in a variety of speakers. It was a highlight of the year for us. People came from all parts of the United States.

On one of these occasions we heard that through prayer a person having diabetes was completely healed. They said an evil spirit was at the root of this illness. This was shocking to us. It had never entered our minds, nor had we ever read or heard of this being possible. We had accepted the medical diagnosis for my husband.

I tucked this information on the back burner in my mind, not ruling it out, but waiting on God to work in our lives with a new hope that He would show us His power. We continued to minister at home and had almost forgotten about this finding.

Then in one of our meetings, a spirit surfaced with the name of Diabetes. It confirmed that it was a generational curse on Armour's family. It had developed a kingdom and its location was on the pancreas controlling the amount of insulin being generated in his body.

Scripture on generational curses is found in **Exodus 20:4-6**. This passage describes one of the Ten Commandments, and the description of how God deals with sin.

"You shall not make for yourself an idol in any form of anything in heaven above or on the earth beneath or in the waters below. You shall not bow down to them or worship them; for I, the

LORD your God, am a jealous God, punishing the children for the sin of the fathers to the third and fourth generation of those who hate me, but showing love to a thousand {generations} of those who love me and keep my commandments."

Armour confessed the sins that gave this spirit freedom to follow the family line to another generation.

The LORD heard his prayer renouncing anything that gave Satan ground to inflict him and possible future generations. God does hear our genuine confessions to Him, but note that it is important to complete the process. As you search through the New Testament you will see that JESUS trained his disciples and sent them out with the instructions to cast out devils and lay hands on the sick so they would recover.

The Gospel of **Mark 16** gives us an account of Jesus' last words of instruction to his disciples before He left and ascended to heaven. This is not a suggestion that Jesus gives, but a mandate of what needs to continue for God's plan to be fulfilled for mankind.

"And He said to them, "Go into all the world and preach the gospel to every creation. He who believes and is baptized will be saved; but he who does not believe will be condemned. And these signs will follow those who believe; in my name they will cast out demons; they will speak with new tongues; they will take up serpents; and if they drink anything deadly, it will by no

means hurt them; they will lay hands on sick people, and they will recover."

So then, after the LORD had spoken to them, He was received up into heaven, and sat down at the right hand of God. And they went out and preached everywhere, the LORD working with [them] and confirming the word through the accompanying signs."   *Mark 16:15-20*

We in turn prayed over Armour and took authority over the evil spirits that had attacked his body, simply commanding them to be made whole, to cancel all past, present and future plans to divide and separate, and to finally go where Jesus sends you. You notice at the end of the above verses in Mark 16, it states, **"the LORD worked with them and confirmed His WORD by the signs that accompanied it."** The work of the LORD, as a result of our prayers, was that diabetes could not be found in my husband. We checked with his doctor and he gave Armour additional tests. His comment was, "This is an enigma and just doesn't happen to a patient with a diabetic condition." The doctor changed Armour's chart and gave further instructions that he was not to receive insulin shots anymore. He was healed from this condition. We gave God the glory.

I continue to believe the words in Mark 16 are for today and did not end when the last disciple died. We are today's disciples and we are to take the other end of the baton that Jesus gives us and run with it, until Jesus returns.

There is nothing like freedom.

"Remember your Creator before the **silver cord** is loosed, or the golden bowl is broken, or the pitcher shattered at the fountain, or the wheel broken at the well. Then the dust will return to the earth as it was, and the spirit will return to God who gave it." *Ecclesiastes 12:6-7*

"I drew them with gentle **cords,** with bands of love." *Hosea 11:4*

"For the word of God is living and active. Sharper than any double-edged sword, it penetrates even to dividing s**oul and spirit,** joints and marrow; it judges the thoughts and attitudes of the heart. Nothing in all creation is hidden from God's sight. Everything is uncovered and laid bare before the eyes of him to whom we must give account." *Hebrews 4:12-13*

The LORD is righteous; He has cut in pieces the cords of the wicked.
Psalm 129:4

I drew them with gentle **cords,** with bands of love.
Hosea 11:4a

I know a man in Christ who fourteen years ago was caught up to the third heaven. Whether it was in the body or **out of the body** I do not know – God knows.
2 Corinthians 12:2

The LORD is my shepherd, I shall not want. He makes me to lie down in green pastures; He leads me beside the still waters. **He restores my soul.**
Psalm 23:1-3a

9

Do Not Be Ignorant Of Satan's Devices

By Siola

This topic for a long time has been kept hidden. However, now we are in an age where displeasing activities are exposed in the media, in magazines, universities, and public schools. One of these areas is astral projection. Astral projection is practiced and experienced by a person who is pledged to be an occult participant or is from the New Age Movement. I am only mentioning the most common groups, but I have no doubt that Satan duplicates this training through organizations around the world, under many names. He needs a lot of assistants to do his dirty work since he can only be in one place at a time. Demons and people all over the world have sold their souls to him, not knowing that he is a great deceiver and cannot be trusted.

Once an individual goes through the oaths, rituals and initiations to join an occult group, the unsuspecting new member is exposed to certain requirements in order to prove their allegiance.

One of the many skills presented at the beginning of occult orientation is to learn to astral project. This is where occult members and demons train a person to "soul travel." The soul (mind, will, and emotions) begins to lift, separating itself from the body and leaving the body behind. Sometimes the body is left in a bed, reclining in a chair, or in a circle where the occult group is astral projecting in mass.

A person who is actually projecting is never seen by anyone. Many who have come out of the occult have admitted they were required to travel through the atmosphere in order to maliciously spy on someone's home, business, or meeting. The occult members fill their time placing specific curses on others. They are expected to concentrate on this activity while orders are given from a witch, warlock, priest, or high priestess to prove their allegiance. They are to block, curse, hinder and destroy the plans of others that are trying to do good. I understand that if you are hearing about this for the first time, it can be hard to believe what I am telling you to be true.

Satan motivates people by a sense of power even though this is an abomination to our Heavenly Father. Individuals expect to be rewarded by Satan for doing his bidding through fame, monetary benefits, sex, promotion in the occult, success in business, or whatever seems to be the greatest need of the person at the time. There is a rush from this power and a feeling of control over others.

When my husband and I were Chaplains in the prison, a young man named Brett let me know he wanted an appointment to talk about a traumatic experience. He had recently accepted Jesus Christ into his life but noticed that something from his past was pursuing him. He believed it was a result of living with a witch for a period of time. Brett was certain his sins were forgiven but something was happening to him and it would not go away. It was frightening and out of control. He confessed it to the LORD but it was still there.

In our conversation, we found out that Brett had lived with a witch for a period of time. He began to describe to us what had happened to him. When he was lying in bed in "lock up" for the night, he suddenly felt himself lifting upward, but his body was not going with him. As much as he tried to pull himself back into his body, it would not work. It was not something he wanted to do (I believe that his soul, which is comprised of his mind, will and emotions is what he felt rising up). His soul continued to lift toward the ceiling of his cell leaving his body behind. He could look back and see himself still lying in the prison bed.

Brett's spirit continued to move right through the locked door and down the stairs to the next landing. He could see everything that was going on. All the inmates were in "lock up," and the guards were at the main desk. Brett began yelling at them to get their attention. Since he had committed his life to God and away from past activities, he knew the LORD Jesus would not be pleased with his actions. He moved and screamed but the guards were not aware that he was even there. Brett found he was floating back up the stairs, through the door of his cell, and then he slipped back into his body. He was shaken and crying out for help wanting to have this taken away. He did not want this to happen again.

As we continued to talk, Brett confessed how much he had missed his girlfriend when he first arrived in prison months ago and felt that he couldn't exist without seeing her. He was desperate enough that he was ready to do anything to be with her. I guess when we want something so badly and we do not ask God, Satan hears us and will "help," but he has ulterior motives. I have said, "If you give Satan the tip of your pinky, he will take up to your elbow." Satan heard Brett's cries and answered him by giving him the ability to travel swiftly through the air and arrive at his girlfriend's house.

When Brett would astral project he could not communicate with his girlfriend, but he could see her lying in bed asleep and was temporarily satisfied. He could also see everything in the room but was unable to move any objects.

Brett requested prayer and confessed before the LORD the inappropriate desires that led to his present problems. He took back the ground that was given to Satan and gave it back to the LORD. I proceeded to bind up the spirit of astral projection in Jesus name, and commanded it to be made whole, to cancel all past, present and future plans to divide and separate and to go where Jesus wanted the evil spirit to go. I asked Brett if he felt any lightheadedness, or any feeling of the spirit of astral projection being removed? To my dismay, he said, "No, it isn't gone."

It must have been that Jesus wanted us to have the proper name of this demon in order for it to leave. I didn't know what other name to call it, nor did Brett, so I claimed **James 1:5** which I have done many times when I did not know the answer. This verse says, **"If any of you lack wisdom, let him ask of God, that giveth to all men liberally, and upbraideth not;** (which *means he will not hold back but will generously give more than we asked)* **and it shall be given him."** I asked the LORD to put the name in either Brett's mind or mine. I encouraged Brett who was new at this to wait on God. I urged Brett to tell me if God had given him the name of the spirit, but if God gave it to me, I would reveal it also.

We sat and chatted awhile and after a little time Brett said, "I hear a name in my head but it can't possibly be the name of the demon." I reminded him that if we ask God we must expect an answer and that I was going to follow through with this name. I can see why Brett thought this couldn't be; he said the name was "Obsneezer."

So I bound up the spirit of Obsneezer in Jesus name, and commanded it to be made whole, to cancel all past, present and future plans to divide and separate. It was ordered to, "go where Jesus sends you." I asked Brett if he felt this oppression being removed this time? Brett answered, "Yes, I could sense the weight of it being lifted and suddenly it was gone." In the following years that we served at the prison, Brett never again had a recurrence of astral projection.

Jesus set him free.

Most beginners of soul travel can only be away from their body for an hour or two at a time. They must get back. Those who have been in the occult for many years have earned the power to stay away from their body for a week or more.

My understanding of the book of Ecclesiastes 12:6,7 is that it speaks of the silver cord being broken. At the time of our birth the umbilical cord must be separated from our mother. Similarly, our bodies are attached to God by a silver cord and the only time we as believers are permitted to fly away is when the angels come to cut the silver cord. We then leave our body behind and angels usher our spirit to God, in His timing not ours. I love the verse that says, **"The day of our death is more precious to God than the day of our birth."** *Psalm 116:15*

I believe astral projection is an abomination to God. All occult practices described in Deuteronomy 7 and 18:9-14 are a stench in God's nostrils. He warns us not to partake in them and not to follow the evil practices of the times. Exodus 20 states, "You shall not have any other Gods before me, for I am a jealous God." In other words he will not share his position with anything or anyone.

Through deliverance over the years the LORD has prompted us to pray, "I break all astral projection curses that may be sent toward us right now, in Jesus name. Father, if there is anyone who is of a reprobate mind, we leave the decision to you to cut, sever or burn the silver cord. Please remove all human souls from our midst. Thank you for your protection, in Jesus name."

In Acts 8:26-40, we have the example of God supernaturally relocating Phillip in a good way. God made the decision to transport him from one location to another. Phillip was taken in **full bodily form** to a road where an Ethiopian eunuch was in a chariot reading scripture but needed someone to explain it to him. Phillip ran alongside the chariot and could hear the Ethiopian's frustration. He offered to explain to him what he was reading.

The end result was spectacular. Phillip was invited into the chariot and was able to lead the Ethiopian to the LORD Jesus. In fact, the Ethiopian saw a body of water and wanted to be baptized immediately.

When they came up out of the water Phillip was gone and could not be found. Phillip did not astral project. In this situation, God miraculously transported Phillip's whole body to another city. His assignment from God was short and temporary.

There appears to be more astral projection than what we currently understand, but I will wait for the LORD to explain that to me someday.

Some Christians with sharp spiritual gifts see beyond the scenes of the physical realm and are able to see angels and demons. However, I have not heard of anyone who has seen an astral projected person.

We Christians in the church can no longer keep the blinders on to the evil in the world. Do you believe that if you ignore the enemy he will ignore you? Look at the violence around us. There is a recent story of a young boy who killed his mother by shooting her in the back of her head, and one of a fearful student who carried a weapon to school for protection.

It is not my intent to produce fear in the readers by disclosing these facts, but instead to equip Christians with knowledge, confidence, and the Word of God that Jesus gave the disciples. Success and victory will result.

Many programs on TV go beyond the physical realm into the dark side. Witchcraft is evidenced through contact with the dead, fortune-tellers, fearful stories of werewolves, vampires, and ghosts, etc. It is no longer a secret anymore. You can be taught demonic skills in your own living room. I can no longer keep quiet while witches are invited to high school classrooms and are given a full lecture period to plant seeds while enticing young people to the power source they represent. There is fertile soil in these schools for the students' minds. Power is not on display anywhere else and since they are bored, witchcraft begins to sprout.

Films and books are available to children presenting demonic skills with easy to follow directions on how to cast spells. They send curses to those with whom they are competing and use demonic means to win by blocking and placing obstacles in their way. I have heard of children spending so much time sharpening their skills that they can become more powerful than a veteran witch. All of this is presented through the media in such a playful, non-threatening way that adults have allowed these movies and books in their homes giving their children have easy access.

Once a young person begins to apply the simple directions shown they feel a new surge of power. They have taken the bait and now the depth of a downward spiral begins. Yet, the children believe they are upward bound. This is a counterfeit freedom and opens the gate for demons to come and go in the child's life. The chains of bondage are placed, and the taste for a variety of occult activities will continue to draw increased interest. There is now a hidden pull to the mystical and magical aspects not present before.

The enemy knows he has a legal right to oppress, harass and rob what God has really intended for them. Soon enough the traits of rebellion toward parental authority, teachers, leaders in the community, or pastors begins to surface. Wholesome activities which once were the center of the child's life are set aside. They may appear withdrawn, isolated from former friends, and now lack a desire to read scripture or even go to church. Witchcraft teaches independence and isolation. It makes them feel they don't need God because they have become a god in their own mind. They now have power and control.

An elderly woman I knew in New York City very rarely left her apartment. Her married daughter lived in the apartment next door and assisted and loved her in every way. Talking with her on the phone one day, I asked if she missed being able to go to a store or other parts of the city, perhaps even visit friends and family. She answered, "I don't miss any of those things. I am very content in my apartment. But I look forward to nighttime for that's when I can fly out my window and go where I want to. I have the ability to visit any place I desire."

At this point in her life it was very difficult to convince and teach her of the things the LORD had shown us.

In review:

- Satan introduces those who are newly inducted in the occult to leave their body and travel swiftly to various places and not be spotted.

- God is displeased with occult practices that teach evil, malicious activity to cause injury, robbery from others, even death.

- Astral projection is common today.

- Astral projection is deceitful and opens a gate for deeper interest in other levels of the occult.

- Spiritual Warfare equips you to set a captive free.

- Avoid and destroy books or DVD's in your possession dealing with any aspect of the occult. This will help keep your home free of demons.

- Let us not be ignorant of Satan's devices.

- Jesus can set you free from any bondage.

There is nothing like freedom.

So shall my **Word** be that proceeds out of my mouth, it shall not return unto me void, but it shall accomplish that which I please, and it shall prosper in the thing to which I sent it.   *Isaiah 55:11*

The **Book of the Law** shall not depart from your mouth, but you shall meditate on it day and night that you may observe to do according to all that is written in it, for then you will make your way prosperous, and then you will have good success.   *Joshua 1:8*

He sent his **Word** and healed them.
                         Psalm 107:20

The **Word** of God is active and
lively, sharper than any double-
edged sword, able to cut asunder
joint and marrow, soul and spirit. It
judges the attitudes and the thoughts
of the heart. Nothing can be hidden
from God. Everything must be laid
bare before him to whom we must
give account.   *Hebrews 4:12*

The **Word** makes you wiser than
your enemies and wiser than your
teachers and elders.   *Psalm 119:98-99*

In the beginning was the **Word,** and
the **Word** was with God, and the
Word was God.   *John 1:1*

10

The Word of God

By Siola

The Word of God is alive. It has the power to change your life. It can cause obstacles in your life to disappear such as the pain of rejection, loneliness, and abandonment. You may remember the experience, but not the pain. The Word will lead you out of the tunnel of your past into a glorious open space. We receive from God's Word a hope and a bright future.

Hiding the Word of God in your heart is like forming layers in a nest. Just as birds prepare a nest for their young, the scriptures line our lives with layers of protection. It becomes a comfortable place that you will return to over and over again. This private nesting place is warm and God Himself will feed us there. He will soothe us and provide a place of rest.

The Word of God has cushioned me in times of crisis. God whispers to me through His Word in loving phrases that could only come from the perfect heart of a loving Father.

As you memorize verses and later larger portions, the Word will drop into your spirit as heavenly dew. It is pure and clean and enters deeply and gently into your heart. This seed will blossom – expanding and changing your life.

God's Word is serene, pure, and calm. It enters your soul and cleanses the debris that lines the inner chambers of your life. The Word of God is magnificent; it is a royal deposit coming from heaven to earth. Each verse of scripture is assigned to do a specific work in your life. God's Word is poured out to you and the more Word you assimilate, the more healing you can expect to come to you.

No matter what the Word says, whether it is in genealogies, songs of praise, intriguing love stories, historical facts, prophecies, promises, or revelation of future events, the Word is love.

His Word cannot be erased. It will forever be my guide and my instructor. It will be ever unfolding before me revealing its depths. It is my daily feeding. When I read it, it enters into my life, deep into the crevices of my being as nothing else can.

The Word of God fortifies us in the challenges of life. It never loses its effectiveness. There is nothing in existence like the Word that invisibly engraves God's mark upon you, claiming us for His own.

There is no doubt we are heaven bound when God's scalpel dips into the hardest to reach places and facilitates the turns and changes that must occur in our lives in order for us to be free.

I've fallen in love with the Word of God, I sense the safety, stability, clarity of mind, purpose, and power that comes when I read and delight in His Word. I love His Word. His Word endures forever and the Word is God.

I can only begin to express some of the magnitude and impact of this eternal gift. How important is the Word of God to you? There are many creative ways to be sure you make time to absorb His Word. Let His Word change you forever.

Do you have an area of your life that needs to be healed? Use the Word.

Immersing yourself in the Word increases your wisdom and intelligence. An inmate that could not read at all began to painstakingly study the Word. Within six months, he was reading at a sixth grade level. The Word can lead to promotions and excellence in your field of work.

Remember the Word of God is alive making you vibrant and full of clarity. You will find your life becomes fruitful and others are drawn to you. The people God brings into your life will want to find out what is happening to you.

You will begin to shed dismal thoughts as the Word cheers you on. It also brings surprises into your life. It produces creativity and ideas downloaded from God especially for you.

The Word can change a home of chaos into a peaceful haven. Allow the Word to enter into your life, family, and your nation.

"Finally, brethren, whatever things are true, whatever things [are] noble, whatever things [are] just, whatever things [are] pure, whatever things [are] lovely, whatever things [are] of good

report. If [there is] any virtue and if [there is] anything praiseworthy – meditate on these things." *Philippians 4:8*

We encourage you to read areas of the Bible that you have not read before. Broaden your vision and ignite a passion in your heart.

I never knew God had specific plans for Satan and his followers. I never knew that there was a war in heaven and who was involved. I never knew how much the angelic hosts were involved in our lives.

Reading from the book of Revelation is exciting. Pictures are drawn with words of upcoming and inspiring events.

I recommend you become familiar with these chapters. Satan is not happy when you are informed about his upcoming doom. His intent would be to keep you in the dark about the future. He believes that by doing so he can continue to place fear, doubt and deception in your life, thus interfering with God's plans.

The following passages of scripture are powerful and through much repetition have impacted my life deeply. I encourage you to meditate on these scriptures as well as have an active reading plan that encompasses both the Old and New Testaments. I have used these passages in overcoming the enemy as I intercede and confront the enemy in one who is being oppressed. Prayer sessions in my home involve the use of a large amount of scripture. It is exciting to see God use His Word (the double-edged sword) to tear down strongholds in a person's life. These are some of the portions that the enemy doesn't want to be reminded about and doesn't want to hear. They are warring passages.

All bold and italic emphasis throughout the scripture references in this chapter are mine.

Total Freedom

A Deliverer Is Born
ISAIAH 9:2-7

The people walking in darkness have seen
a great light; on those living in the land of the shadow
of death **a light has dawned.**

You have enlarged the nation and
increased their joy; they rejoice before you
as people rejoice at the harvest, as men
rejoice when dividing the plunder.

For as in the day of Midian's defeat,
you have shattered the yoke
that burden's them, the bar across
their shoulders, the rod of their oppressor.

Every warrior's boot used in battle and every
garment rolled in blood will be destined for
burning, will be fuel for the fire.

**For to us a child is born, to us a son is given,
and the government shall be upon his shoulders.
And he will be called
Wonderful Counselor, Mighty God
Everlasting Father, Prince of Peace.**

Fall of Babylon
REVELATION 18:1-8

With a mighty voice he shouted:
"Fallen! Fallen, is Babylon the Great!
She has become a home for demons
and a haunt for every evil spirit, a haunt for every
unclean and detestable bird.

For all the nations have drunk the
maddening wine of her adulteries. The
kings of the earth, committed adultery
with her, and the merchants of the
earth grew rich from her excessive luxuries."

Then I heard another voice from heaven say;

**"Come out of her, my people,
so that you will not share in her sins,
so that you will not receive any of her
plagues; for her sins are piled up to heaven,
and God has remembered her crimes.**

**Give back to her as she has given;
pay her back double for what she has done.
Mix her a double portion from her own cup.**

**Give her as much torture and grief as the
glory and luxury as she gave herself.
In her heart she boasts,
'I sit as a queen; I am not a widow,
and I will never mourn.'**

Therefore in one day her plagues will overtake her,
death, mourning, and famine.
She will be consumed by fire,
for mighty is the LORD God who judges her."

The Word Of God

God Rescues the Rejected, Broken, Abused Woman
ISAIAH 54:1-17

"Sing, O barren, You [who] have not borne!
Break forth into singing, and cry aloud,
You [who] have not labored with child!
For more [are] the children of the desolate
Than the children of the married woman,"
says the LORD.

"Enlarge the place of your tent,
And let them stretch out the curtains
of your dwellings;
Do not spare; Lengthen your cords,
And strengthen your stakes.

For you shall expand to the right and to
the left, And your descendants will
inherit the nations, And make the
desolate cities inhabited.

"Do not fear, for you will not be ashamed; Neither be
disgraced, for you will
not be put to shame;
For you will forget the shame of your youth,
And will not remember the reproach of
your widowhood anymore.

For your Maker [is] your husband,
The LORD of hosts [is] His name;
And your Redeemer [is] the Holy One of Israel;
He is called the God of the whole earth.

Total Freedom

For the LORD has called you like a woman
forsaken and grieved in spirit,
Like a youthful wife when you were refused,"
Says your God.

"For a mere moment I have forsaken you,
But with great mercies I will gather you.

With a little wrath I hid My face
from you for a moment;
But with everlasting kindness
I will have mercy on you,"
Says the LORD," your Redeemer.

"For this [is] like the waters of Noah to Me;
For as I have sworn, That the waters of Noah
would no longer cover the earth,
So have I sworn That I would not be angry
with you, nor rebuke you.

For the mountains shall depart And the
hills be removed, But My kindness shall not depart from
you, Nor shall My covenant of peace be removed,"
Says the LORD,
who has mercy on you.

"O you afflicted one, Tossed with tempest, [and] not
comforted, Behold, I will lay your stones with colorful
gems, And lay your foundations with sapphires.

I will make your pinnacles of rubies, Your gates of
crystal, And all your walls of precious stones.

The Word Of God

All your children [shall be]
taught by the LORD, And great [shall be]
the peace of your children.

In righteousness you shall be established;
You shall be far from oppression, for you
shall not fear; And from terror, for it
shall not come near you.

Indeed they shall surely assemble, [but] not because
of Me. Whoever assembles
against you shall fall for your sake.

"Behold, I have created the blacksmith
Who blows the coals in the fire,
Who brings forth an instrument for his work;
And I have created the spoiler to destroy.

No weapon formed against you shall prosper, And
every tongue [which] rises against you in judgment
You shall condemn. This [is] the heritage of the
servants of the LORD, And their righteousness [is] from
Me," Says the LORD.

God's Angels Prepare a Way for You
EXODUS 23: 20-30

See, I am sending an angel ahead of you to guard you along the way and to bring you to the place I have prepared. Pay attention to him and listen to what he says. Do not rebel against him, he will not forgive your rebellion, since my Name is in him.

If you listen carefully to what he says
and do all that I say,

**I will be an enemy to your enemies
and oppose them who oppose you.**

My angel will go ahead of you and bring you into the land of the Amorites, Hittites, Perrizites, Canaanites, Hivites, and Jebusites, and I will wipe them out. Do not bow down before their gods or worship them or follow their practices. You must demolish them and break their sacred stones to pieces.

Worship the LORD your God, and the blessing will be on your food and water.

**I will take sickness from among you,
and none will miscarry and be barren in your land. I
will give you a full life span.**

"I will send my terror ahead of you and throw into confusion every nation you encounter.
I will make all of your enemies turn their backs and run.
I will send the hornet ahead of you
to drive the Hivites, Canaanites, and
Hittites out of your way.

The Word Of God

But I will not drive them out in a single year, because the land will become desolate and the wild animals too numerous for you.

Little by little I will drive them out before you, until you have increased enough to take possession of the land."

Satan's Doom
REVELATION 20:7-10

When the thousand years are over, Satan will be
released from his prison and will go out to deceive the
nations in the four corners of the earth -- Gog and
Magog -- to gather them
for battle. In number they are like
the sand on the seashore.

They marched across the breadth of the earth
and surrounded the camp of God's people,
the city he loves.

**But fire came down from heaven
and devoured them.
And the devil, who deceived them,
was thrown into the lake of burning sulfur,
where the beast and the false prophet
had been thrown.**

They will be tormented day and night
forever and ever.

Taking the Mark Results In Torment and No Rest

REVELATION 14:9-12

Then a third angel followed them, saying with a loud voice, "If anyone worships the beast and his image, and receives [his] mark on his forehead or on his hand,

"He himself shall also drink of the wine of the wrath of God, which is poured out full strength into the cup of His indignation. He shall be tormented with fire and brimstone in the presence of the holy angels and in the presence of the Lamb.

"And the smoke of their torment ascends forever and ever; **and they have no rest day or night, who worship the beast and his image, and whoever receives the mark of his name." Here is the patience of the saints; here [are] those who keep the commandments of God and the faith of Jesus.**

The Lord Fights Our Battle
ISAIAH 22:17-19

Beware the LORD is about to take firm hold of you and
hurl you away, O you mighty man.

He will roll you up tightly like a ball
and throw you into a large country.
There you will die and there your
splendid chariots will remain –

You disgrace to your master's house.

**I will depose you from your office,
and you will be ousted from your position.**

The Word Of God

Urgent Warning Not to Practice Casting Spells, Divination, Witchcraft, Sorcery, Medium or Spirits

DEUTERONOMY 18:9-14

When you come into the land which the LORD your God is giving you, you shall not learn to follow the abominations of those nations.

There shall not be found among you [anyone] who makes his son or his daughter pass through the fire, [or one] who practices witchcraft, [or] a soothsayer, or one who interprets omens, or a sorcerer, or one who conjures spells, or a medium, or a spiritist, or one who calls up the dead.

For all who do these things [are] an abomination to the LORD, and because of these abominations the LORD your God drives them out from before you.

You shall be blameless before the LORD you God. For these nations which you will dispossess listened to soothsayers and diviners; but as for you, the LORD your God has not appointed such for you.

We are Over-Comers
REVELATION 12:7-12

And there was war in heaven. Michael and
his angels fought against the dragon, and the dragon
and his angels fought back. But
he was not strong enough, and
they lost their place in heaven.

The great dragon was hurled down, that ancient
serpent called the devil, or Satan,
who leads the whole world astray. He was hurled to
the earth, and his angels with him.

Then I heard a loud voice in heaven say:

"Now have come the salvation and the
power and the kingdom of our God, and the
authority of his Christ. For the accuser of our brothers,
who accuses them before our God day and night,
has been hurled down.

They overcame him by the blood of the Lamb and
the word of their testimony; they did not love their lives
so much as to shrink from
death. Therefore rejoice, you heavens and you who
dwell in them! But woe to the earth and the sea,
because the devil has gone down
to you! He is filled with fury because he
knows that his time is short."

The Word Of God

Time for Everything

ECCLESIASTES 3:1-11a

There is a time for everything,
and a season for every activity under heaven:

a time to be born and a time to die,
a time to plant and a time to uproot,

a time to kill and a time to heal,
a time to tear down and a time to build up,

a time to weep and a time to laugh,
a time to mourn and a time to dance,

a time to scatter stones and a time to gather them, a
time to embrace and a time to refrain,

a time to search and a time to give up,
a time to keep and a time to throw away,

a time to tear and a time to mend,
a time to be silent and a time to speak,

a time to love and a time to hate,
a time for war and a time for peace.

What does the worker gain from his toil?
I have seen the burden God has laid on me.
He has made everything beautiful in His time.

Rider on the White Horse
REVELATION 19:11-16

I saw heaven standing open
and there before me was a white horse,
whose rider is called faithful and true.
With justice he judges and makes war.

His eyes are like blazing fire,
and on his head are many crowns.
He has a name written on him that no one
knows but he himself. He is dressed in
a robe dipped in blood, and his
name is the **Word of God.**

The armies of heaven were following him,
riding on white horses and dressed in
fine linen, white and clean.

Out of his mouth comes a sharp sword with which to
strike down the nations. He will rule them with an iron
scepter. He treads the winepress of the fury of the
God Almighty. On his robe and on his thigh he has his
name written: **KING OF KINGS AND LORD OF LORDS**

The Word Of God

Satan Loses His Position In Heaven
ISAIAH 14:12-17

How you have fallen from heaven
O Morning Star, son of the dawn!
You have been cast down to the earth,
You who once laid low the nations!

You said in your heart,
I will ascend into heaven;
I will raise my throne above the stars of God;
I will sit enthroned on the mount of assembly,
on the utmost heights of the sacred mountain.
I will ascend above the tops of the clouds;
I will make myself like the Most High.

But you are brought down to the grave,
to the depths of the pit. Those who see you stare at
you, they ponder your fate:
"Is this the man who shook the earth
and made the kingdoms tremble,
the man who made the world a desert,
who overthrew its cities,
and would not let his captives go home?"

Total Freedom

God Fights for Me
PSALM 35: 4-13

May those who seek my life be disgraced
and put to shame; may those who plot my
ruin be turned back in dismay.

May they be like chaff before the wind,
with the **angel of the LORD** driving them away;
may their path be dark and slippery,
with the **angel of the LORD** pursuing them.

Since they had their net for me without
cause and without cause dug a pit for me,
may ruin overtake them by surprise --
may the net they hid entangle them,
may they fall into the pit, to their ruin.

**Then my soul will rejoice in the LORD
and delight in his salvation.
My whole being will exclaim,
"Who is like you, O LORD?"
You rescue the poor from those too
strong for them, the poor and needy
from those who rob them."**

The Word Of God

Prayer of Faith
JAMES 5:13-19

Is anyone of you in trouble? He should pray. Is anyone happy? Let him sing songs of praise. Is anyone of you sick? He should call for the elders of the church to pray over him and anoint him with oil in the name of the Lord.

And the prayer offered in faith will make the sick person well; the Lord will raise him up. If he has sinned he will be forgiven. Therefore confess your sins to each other and pray for each
other that you may be healed.

**The prayer of a righteous man is powerful
and effective.**

Elijah was a man just like us. He prayed earnestly that it would not rain, and it did not rain on the land for three and a half years. Again he prayed, and the heavens gave rain, and the earth produced its crops. My brothers, if anyone of you should wander from the truth and someone should bring him back.

Remember this: **Whoever turns a sinner from the error of his way will save him from death and cover a multitude of sins.**

Collection of God's Promises
PSALM 91

He who dwells in the secret
place of the Most High
Shall abide under the shadow of the
Almighty. I will say of the LORD,
"*He is* my refuge and my fortress;
My God, in Him I will trust."

Surely He shall deliver you from the
snare of the fowler.
And from the perilous pestilence.
He shall cover you with His feathers,
And under His wings you shall take refuge;
His truth *shall be your* shield and buckler.

You shall not be afraid of the terror by night,
Nor of the arrow *that* flies by day,
Nor of the pestilence *that* walks in
darkness, *Nor* of the destruction *that*
lays waste at noonday.

A thousand may fall at your side,
And ten thousand at your right hand;
But it shall not come near you.
Only with your eyes shall you look,
And see the reward of the wicked.

Because you have made the LORD, *who is* my refuge,
Even the Most High, your dwelling place,

The Word Of God

No evil shall befall you,
Nor shall any plague come near your
dwelling; For He shall give His
angels charge over you,
To keep you in all your ways.
In *their* hands they shall bear you up,
Lest you dash your foot against a stone.
You shall tread upon the lion and the cobra,
The young lion and the serpent you
shall trample underfoot.

"Because he has set his love upon Me,
therefore I will deliver him.
I will set him on high, because he
has known My name.

He shall call upon Me, and I will answer him;
I *will be* with him in trouble;
I will deliver him and honor him.
With long life I will satisfy him,
And show him My salvation."

Blow the Trumpet
JOEL 2:1-11

**Blow the trumpet in Zion;
sound the alarm on my Holy Hill.**

Let all who live in the land tremble, for the day of the
LORD is coming.   It is close at hand-
a day of darkness and gloom,
a day of clouds and blackness,
like dawn spreading across the mountains
a large and mighty army comes, such as never was of
old nor ever will be in ages to come.

Before them fire devours, behind them a flame blazes.
Before them the land is like the Garden of Eden,
behind them, a desert waste, nothing escapes them.

They have the appearance of horses;
they gallop along like cavalry.
With a noise like that of chariots
they leap over the mountaintops,
like a crackling fire consuming stubble,
like a mighty army drawn for battle.

At the sight of them, nations are in anguish;
every face turns pale. They charge like warriors,
they scale walls like soldiers.
They all march in line, not
swerving from their course.

The Word Of God

They do not jostle each other; each marches
straight ahead. They plunge through
defenses without breaking ranks,
They rush upon the city; they run along
the wall. They climb into the houses;
Like thieves they enter through the windows
Before them the earth shakes, the sky trembles
The sun and moon are darkened, and
the stars no longer shine.

The LORD thunders at the head of his army
His forces are beyond number
and mighty are those who obey his command.
The day of the LORD is great;
Who can endure it?

"Even now, declares the LORD, return to me with all
your heart, with fasting and weeping and mourning.
Rend your heart
and not your garments.
Return to the LORD your God,
for he is gracious and compassionate,
slow to anger and abounding in love,
and he relents from sending calamity.
Who knows? He may turn and have pity and leave
behind a blessing - grain offerings and drink offerings
for the LORD your God.

Blow the trumpet in Zion, declare a holy fast,
call a sacred assembly. Gather the people
Consecrate the assembly; Bring together
the elders Gather the children,
those nursing at the breast.

Let the bridegroom leave his room and the bride her chamber. Let the priests who minister before the LORD weep between the temple porch and the altar. Let them say "Spare your people, O LORD. Do not make your inheritance an object of scorn, a byword among the nations. Why should they say among the peoples, Where is their God?"

The Word Of God

Scripture to Use Against the Enemy

Jesus said to him, "It is written..." *Matthew 4:7a*

And it shall come to pass [That] whoever calls on the name of the LORD Shall be saved. *Acts 2:21*

Submit yourselves, then, to God. Resist the devil, and he will flee from you. *James 4:7*

Upon the wicked it shall rain snares, fire and brimstone, and an horrible tempest: [this shall be] the portion of their cup. *Psalm 11:6*

For the word of God is living and active. Sharper than any double-edged sword, it penetrates even to dividing soul and spirit, joints and marrow; it judges the thoughts and attitudes of the heart. *Hebrews 4:12-13*

The wicked are overthrown and [are] not, but the house righteous will stand. *Proverbs 12:7*

The name of the LORD is a strong tower; the righteous run to it and are safe. *Proverbs 18:10*

Who is this King of glory? The Lord strong and mighty, the Lord mighty in battle. *Psalm 24:8*

Total Freedom

All those gathered here will know that it is not by sword or spear that the LORD saves; for the battle is the Lord's.   *I Samuel 17:47a*

I am the Lord and there is none else.   *Isaiah 45:6b*

For God has not given us a spirit of fear, but of power and of love and of a sound mind.   *2 Timothy 1:7*

I sought the LORD, and he heard me, And delivered me from all my fears.   *Psalm 34:4*

This poor man called, and the LORD heard him; he saved him out of all his troubles.   *Psalm 34:6*

Many are the afflictions of the righteous, But the LORD delivers him out of them all.   *Psalm 34:19*

God is our refuge and strength, A **very present help** in trouble.   *Psalm 46:1b*

The LORD is my light and my salvation--Whom shall I fear? The LORD is the stronghold of my life--of whom shall I be afraid?   *Psalm 27:1*

Yea, though I walk through the valley of the shadow of death, I will fear no evil: for thou art with me; thy rod and thy staff they comfort me.   *Psalm 23:4*

The Lord shall preserve thee from all evil: he shall preserve thy soul.   *Psalm 121:7*

The Lord shall preserve thy going out and thy coming in from this time forth, and even for evermore.
                                                            Psalm 121:8

But if I with the finger of God cast out devils, no doubt the kingdom of God is come upon you.   *Luke 11:20*

When a strong man, fully armed, guards his own palace, his goods are in peace. "But when a stronger than he comes upon him and overcomes him, he takes from him all his armor in which he trusted, and divides his spoils.   *Luke 11:21,22*

He who is not with me is against me, and he who does not gather with me scatters.   *Matthew 12:30*

But the wicked shall perish, and the enemies of the LORD [shall be] as the fat of the lambs: they shall consume; into smoke shall they consume away.
                                                            Psalm 37:20

And God is **angry** [with the wicked] every day.
                                                            Psalm 7:11b

He made a pit and dug it out, And has fallen into the ditch [which] he made.   *Psalm 7:15*

His mischief shall return upon his own head.
Psalm 7:16a

And God placed all things under his feet...
Ephesians 1:22a

And God raised us up with Christ and seated us with him in the heavenly realms in Christ Jesus.
Ephesians 2:6

Thou hast rebuked the heathen, thou hast destroyed the wicked, thou hast put out their name for ever and ever.
Psalm 9:5

Jesus looked at them and said, "With man this is impossible, but with God all things are possible."
Matthew 19:26

Verily, verily, I say unto you, He that believeth on me, the works that I do shall he do also; and greater [works] than these shall he do; because I go unto My Father.
John 14:12

And whatsoever ye shall ask in my name, that will I do, that the Father may be glorified in the Son. *John 14:13*

Jesus Christ is the same yesterday and today and forever.
Hebrews 13:8

The Word Of God

You are of God, little children, and have overcome them, because He who is in you is greater than he who is in the world.   *1 John 4:4*

For verily I say unto you, That whosoever shall say unto this mountain, Be thou removed, and be thou cast into the sea; and shall not doubt in his heart, but shall believe that those things which he saith shall come to pass; he shall have whatsoever he saith.   *Mark 11:23*

Therefore I say unto you, What things soever ye desire, when ye pray, believe that ye receive [them] and ye shall have [them].   *Mark 11:24*

So is My Word that goes forth out of My mouth; It will not return to me empty, but will accomplish what I desire and achieve the purpose for which I sent it.
Isaiah 55:11

And when He had called unto [him] his twelve disciples, he gave them power [against] unclean spirits, to cast them out, and to heal all manner of sickness and all manner of disease.   *Matthew 10:1*

And as ye go, preach, saying, The kingdom of heaven is at hand. **Heal the sick, cleanse the lepers, raise the dead, cast out devils: freely ye have received, freely give**.   *Matthew 10:7,8*

Behold, I give unto you power to tread on serpents and scorpions, and over **all** the power of the enemy: and **nothing shall by any means hurt you**.   *Luke 10:19*

Who through faith subdued kingdoms, wrought righteousness, obtained promises, stopped the mouths of lions, Quenched the violence of fire, escaped the edge of the sword, out of weakness were made strong, waxed valiant in fight, turned to flight the armies of the aliens.   *Hebrews 11:33,34*

Scripture to Combat Fear

And the officers shall speak further to the people, and shall say, "What man [is there who is] **fearful** and **fainthearted**? Let him go and return to his house, lest the heart of his brethren **faint** like his heart.
                    Deuteronomy 20:8

Yea, though I walk through the valley of the shadow of death, I will **fear** no evil; For you [are] with me; Your rod and Your staff, they comfort me.   *Psalm 23:4*

The LORD is my light and my salvation; Whom shall I **fear**? The LORD [is] the strength of my life; Of whom shall I be **afraid**? Though an army may encamp against me, My heart shall not **fear**; Though war may rise against me, In this I [will be] confident.
                    Psalm 27:1,3

I sought the Lord, and he heard me, And delivered me from all my **fears.**   *Psalm 34:4*

God [is] our refuge and strength, A very present help in trouble. Therefore we will not **fear**, Even though the earth be removed, And though the mountains be carried into the midst of the sea.   *Psalm 46:1,2*

Wherefore should I **fear** in the days of evil, [when] the iniquity of my heels shall compass me about?
Psalm 49:5

Hear my voice, O God, in my prayer: preserve my life from **fear** of the enemy.   *Psalm 64:1*

The Lord [is] on my side; I will not **fear**: what can man do unto me?   *Psalm 118:6*

But whoever listens to me shall dwell safely, And will be secure, without **fear** of evil.   *Proverb 1:33*

Be not afraid of sudden **fear**, neither of the desolation of the wicked, when it cometh.   *Proverb 3:25*

Say to them [that are] of a **fearful** heart, Be strong, **fear not:** behold, your God will come [with] vengeance, [even] God [with] a recompense; he will come and save you.   *Isaiah 35:4*

And **fear not** them which kill the body, but are not able to kill the soul: but rather fear him which is able to destroy both soul and body in hell.   *Matthew 10:28*

For ye have not received the spirit of bondage again to **fear**; but ye have received the Spirit of adoption, whereby we cry, Abba, Father.   *Romans 8:15*

For God has not given us the spirit of **<u>fear</u>**, but of power and of love and of a sound mind.   *2 Timothy 1:7*

Forasmuch then as the children are partakers of flesh and blood, he also himself likewise took part of the same; that through death he might destroy him that had the power of death, that is, the devil; And deliver them who through **<u>fear of death</u>** were all their lifetime subject to bondage.   *Hebrews 2:14-15*

There is no **<u>fear</u>** in love; but perfect love casts out **<u>fear</u>**, because **<u>fear</u>** involves torment. But he who **<u>fears</u>** has not been made perfect in love.   *I John 4:18*

Scripture for Deliverance

The LORD shall **preserve** you from all evil: He shall **preserve** your soul.   *Psalm 121:7*

The LORD [is] a **man of war:** The LORD [is] his name.   *Exodus15:3*

The **wicked are overthrown,** and [**are**] **not:** but the house of the righteous shall stand.   *Proverbs 12:7*

Upon the wicked he shall rain **snares, fire** and **brimstone,** and an horrible **tempest;** [this shall be] the portion of their cup.   *Psalm 11:6*

The Word Of God

The name of the LORD [is] a **strong tower;** The righteous run to it and are **safe.** *Proverbs 18:10*

The LORD **strong** and **mighty,** the LORD **mighty in battle.** *Psalm 24:8b*

I sought the LORD, and he heard me, And **delivered** me from **ALL** my **fears.** *Psalm 34:4*

And all this assembly shall know that the LORD saveth not with the sword and the spear: for the **battle [is] the LORD'S**, and he will give you into our hands. *I Samuel 17:47*

For God hath not given us the **spirit of fear;** but of **power,** and of **love,** and of a **sound mind.** *1 Timothy 4:7*

Behold, I give unto you **power** to **tread** on serpents and scorpions, and over **ALL the power of the enemy,** and nothing shall by any means hurt you. *Luke 10:19*

He shall say, "Hear, O Israel, today you are going into battle against your enemies. **Do not be fainthearted or afraid; do not be terrified or give way to panic before them. For the LORD your God is the one who goes with you to fight for you against your enemies to give you the victory.** *Deuteronomy 20:3*

No one will be able to stand against you all the days of your life. As I was with Moses, **so I will be with you; I will never leave you nor forsake you.** *Joshua 1:5*

But to you that fear My name The Sun of Righteousness shall arise With healing in His wings; And you shall go out And grow fat like stall-fed calves. **You shall trample** the wicked.   *Malachi 4:2,3a*

The LORD [is] good, a **strong hold** in the **day of trouble.**   *Nahum 1:7a*

Yet in all these things we are **more than conquerors** through Him who loved us.   *Romans 8:37*

Submit yourselves therefore to God. **Resist** the devil, and **he will flee from you.**   *James 4:7*

Many [are] the afflictions of the righteous, But the LORD **delivers** him out of them **ALL.**   *Psalm 34:19*

Ye are of God, little children, **and have overcome them:** because **greater is he that is in you, than he that is in the world.**   *I John 4:4*

And when he had called unto [him] his twelve disciples, He gave them **power [against] unclean spirits,** to cast them out, and to heal **ALL manner of sickness and ALL manner of disease.**   *Matthew 10:1*

The LORD [is] my light and my salvation, **whom then shall I fear?** The LORD [is] the strength of my life; **of whom shall I be afraid?**   *Psalm 27:1*

The Word Of God

For he has **delivered me from ALL my troubles,** and my eyes have looked in **triumph** on my foes. *Psalm 54:7*

Through God **we shall do valiantly:** for he [it is that] shall **tread down our enemies.** *Psalm 60:12*

Say unto God, How terrible [art thou in] thy works! through the greatness of the power shall thine enemies **submit themselves unto thee.** *Psalm 66:3*

The angel of the LORD **encamps round** all around **those** who fear Him, And **delivers them.** *Psalm 34:7*

A righteous man may have many troubles, but the LORD **delivers him from them all.** *Psalm 34:19*

Have I not commanded you? Be strong and courageous. **Do not be terrified; do not be discouraged,** for the LORD your God will **be with you wherever you go.** *Joshua 1:9*

Don't be afraid of them, Remember the LORD, who is great and awesome, and **fight for your brothers, your sons and your daughters, your wives and your homes.** *Nehemiah 4:14b*

Who through **faith** subdued kingdoms, wrought righteousness, obtained promises, stopped the mouths of lions, quenched the violence of fire, escaped the edge of the sword, out of weakness were made strong, waxed valiant in fight, turned to flight the armies of the aliens. *Hebrews 11:33-34*

Appendix A

Rearrange Your World

Every word we speak affects the world around us. Words are powerful and creative. God hears them, angels hear them, and demons also hear them. When we speak, a gate is opened and what has been stated is released.

As a young pastor's wife, I remember spotting a book on my husband's desk titled, "What You Say is What You Get," by Don Gossett. When we speak words based on God's Word, blessings are released from heaven. Our Heavenly Father commands angels to deposit and affect the world in which we live. The havoc we experience in our lives may be a result of the way we speak about things around us.

The following declarations can be used and are most powerful when stated out loud at the beginning of everyday. When we develop a pattern of expectancy in our minds and when our words agree with God's Word, we will begin to experience positive changes.

Create Your Own Declarations of Faith.

I am blessed

I cast all my cares upon you

I am the head and not the tail

Total Freedom

I will not park in the past

I am doing all right

I will fight the good fight of faith

I am coming up and coming over

I will become better

The LORD is my portion

I am adequate

I am complete

I will not be afraid

I am a learner

I am strong

Financial blessings are coming my way

I am going over and not under

My house is a blessed house

My children will rise up and be successful

My children are blessed children

The devil cannot have my family, body, or my mind

I claim my family to be saved

I will say of the LORD, He is my refuge and fortress

I can do all things through Christ's strength

By His stripes I am healed

I claim the blessings of the seed of Abraham

My mind is alert

My body is strong

I am getting stronger everyday

I have a good memory

Friends are moving in my direction

The spirit of God is rising up inside of me

Total Freedom

My discernment is working

I am satisfied with what I have

I will not complain and argue as I go about my day

I will not allow wicked or evil things before my eyes

I have favor with God and man

I am peaceful when I go to sleep

I will not be anxious, but full of thanksgiving to God

I guard my mouth and tongue

I keep my soul from troubles

I surround myself with wise people

I love God's word, I think about it all day long

I listen to counsel, and receive instruction

I am quick to listen, slow to speak and slow to anger

The words that I speak are spirit and life

Appendix B

Phrases To Assist In Warfare Praying

When praying in a deliverance session, we have found the following key phrases and concepts to be powerful during prayer. They are reminders of what we can pray and how we can ask God to send angels to fight on our behalf.

Angels of war to be released

Liberty to be released

Break bands of prayerlessness

Call for wrecking balls of fire

Utterance come forth now

Spirit of disobedient children be smashed now

May the warpath of God be enlarged now

Concentration of devils be broken apart

Loosen missiles in the spirit

Total Freedom

Weapons of warfare

Perseverance to pray

Smash the throne of schizophrenia

Let the battering ram of the LORD come in

Access at the gates to everything that has been denied

Break spirits of religion, Babylon, Nimrod

Command (take authority) over the spirit of religion

Bind the hands of Lucifer over the city, townships, suburbs, county, country and state

Bring down the walls of denominationalism

Break psychic activity over the city, townships, county, country, state

Break the spirit of witchcraft

Acknowledgements

I want to thank all the warriors who have joined Armour and me in holding our position on the battlefield throughout the years. We have learned together as we have come alongside many who have needed assistance and needed family.

To all whose efforts, encouragement, and commitment to the vision that made the ministry of Total Freedom Fellowship possible, I would like to personally thank Todd Eklund, Jim Dykens, John Krupczak, David Szymas, Andy Garsed, Joanne Warren, Barb Norlin, June Barber, Evelyn Rodriquez, Betty Castro, Natasha Smith, Josie Vela Rose, Sharon Overbeek, Darlene Wabeke, and numerous others. You have been faithful partners in the ministry placed before us, never wavering in faith. My life is blessed because of your friendship and willingness to help rescue people from the pit.

Thank you also to Heidi Harrington for your creative design on the book cover and to Scott McFarland for assisting in scripture research.

The completion of this book would not have been possible without the efforts of Terri McFarland and Tracy Hanson who committed countless hours to the editing process. Thank you for your belief in me, in the call on my life, and in the vision for this book.

Most importantly, my heart overflows with gratitude to my Lord and Savior Jesus Christ who has loved me and led me, and to the precious Holy Spirit who patiently guided Armour and me through this wonderful journey. I long for the day when I see you face to face.